Pete Buckley ru
easywayup.com and
further afield. He is the author of 57 Days in a Van, recounting a journey around New Zealand made during the summer of 2005 and *A Long Walk in the Alps* which is his second book. He lives in the Blackburn area, is married to Jacqui and has two sons, Josh aged 10 years and Daniel aged 7 days at the time of writing.

Also by Pete Buckley

31 Days in a Campervan is the story of a journey around New Zealand made in the summer of 2005. Travelling by campervan is arguably the best way to see this amazing country and the route itself is perhaps one of the best journeys in the World. If your love is for nature, the outdoors and the freedom of the open spaces, then this is a must! Paperback 149 pages ISBN 142512183-7

A Long Walk in The Alps

From the Eiger to the Matterhorn

By Pete Buckley

Order this book online at www.trafford.com/08-0075
or email orders@trafford.com

Most Trafford titles are also available at major online book retailers.

© Copyright 2008 Pete Buckley.

All rights reserved. No part of this publication may be reproduced, stored in a retrieval system, or transmitted, in any form or by any means, electronic, mechanical, photocopying, recording, or otherwise, without the written prior permission of the author.

Note for Librarians: A cataloguing record for this book is available from Library and Archives Canada at www.collectionscanada.ca/amicus/index-e.html

ISBN: 978-1-4251-6781-3

We at Trafford believe that it is the responsibility of us all, as both individuals and corporations, to make choices that are environmentally and socially sound. You, in turn, are supporting this responsible conduct each time you purchase a Trafford book, or make use of our publishing services. To find out how you are helping, please visit www.trafford.com/responsiblepublishing.html

Our mission is to efficiently provide the world's finest, most comprehensive book publishing service, enabling every author to experience success. To find out how to publish your book, your way, and have it available worldwide, visit us online at www.trafford.com/10510

 www.trafford.com

North America & international
toll-free: 1 888 232 4444 (USA & Canada)
phone: 250 383 6864 ♦ fax: 250 383 6804 ♦ email: info@trafford.com

The United Kingdom & Europe
phone: +44 (0)1865 722 113 ♦ local rate: 0845 230 9601
facsimile: +44 (0)1865 722 868 ♦ email: info.uk@trafford.com

10 9 8 7 6 5 4 3 2 1

The maps on the following pages show the approximate route taken. Please note that these maps are for reference whilst reading the story and are not suitable for navigating one's way through the mountains. That is, of course, unless the aim is a ride in the rescue helicopter and that is a very expensive way to see Switzerland. Far cheaper and more useful to navigation are the Kummerley and Frey maps (No 18 – Jungfrau Region and No 24 – Zermatt/Saas Fee) I used on the walk.

The total distance from Grindelwald to Zermatt is up to the individual who can decide whether to follow the route taken or any of the variations and how much to cheat and get the bus. Indeed the easiest option is to read the book from the comfort of an armchair which ideally has close proximity to an open bottle of wine. All the distances, details and variations are noted on easywayup.com as are lots of other rewarding routes much shorter than this one.

Big thanks as well to Jacqui and her mum Val who did most of the typing as I'd have been here another month with my 2 fingered, super snail speed typing skills.

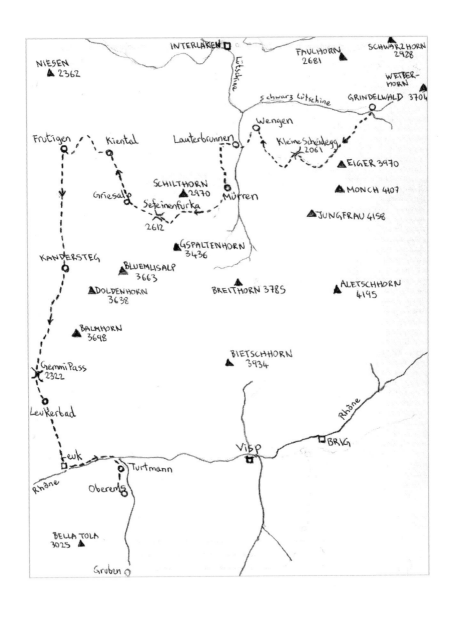

Map 1 - from Grindelwald to the Rhone

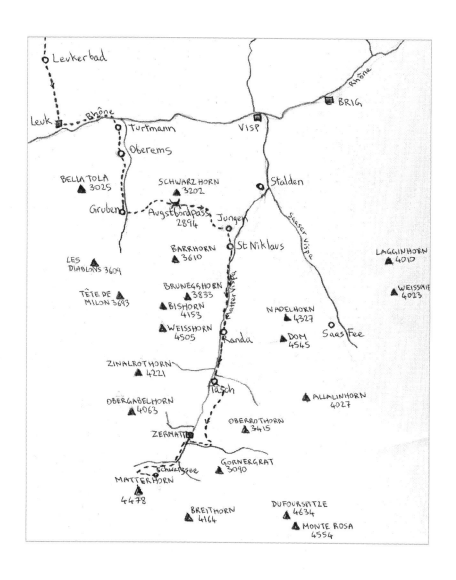

Map 2 – from the Rhone to Zermatt

Contents

Introduction

(1) A New Route in the Alps

(2) From Blackburn to the Bernese Oberland

(3) Friday 13th on the Eiger

(4) Smoked Salmon for Breakfast

(5) Into the Wilds

(6) A Lone Red Kite

(7) Walking Off the Map

(8) A Chill in the Morning Air

(9) In the Valley of the Matterhorn

(10) The Europaweg

(11) The Long Walk Home

Introduction

  Leaving my ski poles in an upright "V" position, I settled down to wait for the snow cat that would take me back down to Plan de Jeux. It would be dark in an hour and sleety snow gusted across the mountainside while the higher peaks merged into the iron grey ceiling just above. I tightened my hood against the rising wind.

  My knee no longer hurt now that I was sat down but the effort of trying to make turns on skis had risked worsening the injury and though I protested that I could have walked or at least limped down the slope, I felt a secret relief that the effort was over. I know that effectively being rescued when I wasn't that badly hurt was like giving up but my instructor had said that a lift down was no trouble to anyone and given the lateness of the hour, she was probably right. Besides – I had never been on a snow cat and was quite looking forward to it.

  Looking around I began to appreciate my surroundings a bit more. Alone, five thousand feet up a mountain, in rapidly deteriorating weather and approaching twilight – I was warm though and Plan de Jeux was little more than a mile away so my situation didn't unnerve me. The only sound was the wind brushing the snow against my hood and jacket, any other noises there might have been in the forest were lost in the white swirling mass. Below through the trees, the faint lights of the village were starting to appear and much further down, the dark valley of the Rhone was almost lost from view as the winter darkness approached.

This was my first time in the Alps in winter and I tried to imagine these hills above Torgon in the summer, green meadows dotted with grazing cattle and forest trails leading up to breezy summits with far off views. It would make good walking country this. Gradually, I became aware of a noise above the wind. It became louder, cutting through the muffling snow, rising and falling in strident tones – an engine. Then the lights appeared through the trees and I waved to the driver of the snow cat. My taxi had arrived.

Chapter One
A New Route in the Alps

As the rain battered the window violently and Winter Hill once again disappeared from view behind the squalls, I thought back to the skiing trip and felt a sense of relief that the injury had been minor. I could have been sat here writing a story called "Great Train Journeys of Switzerland" or something similar. The English Summer was now upon us and I'd be back in the Alps in a little over a month

The injury, while confirming my initial opinion – that skiing is dangerous – had turned out to be nothing worse than a bad sprain and the Glacier Express would have to wait until another time. Seriously though, I had enjoyed my first efforts at skiing and was maybe lucky to get away with nothing worse than a sprained knee. The sport is surely a more dignified way of descending a hill than on one's backside although that same backside has a lot further to fall from a standing up position.

It had been for some time now that I'd been thinking about doing a decent sized trek in the Alps, my experience so far consisting only of day hikes and easy summits. I was after doing a trip that could be done by any reasonably fit hiker in a normal fortnight's holiday without having to walk 20 miles a day or risk winding up at the bottom of a crevasse. Just a look on the internet or in any hiking magazine reveals an endless list of possibilities – Chamonix to Zermatt by a choice of Haute Routes, the Tour du Mont Blanc (TMB), the Alpine Pass Route, the Oberland Haute Route as well as the Tour of Monte Rosa, the Circuit of the Matterhorn and many more. You can go in a group, self guided, backpacking, hut to hut, in hotels or on bike! Such is the level of choice available. I immediately thought however that it would add to the excitement if I could come up with my own route.

Coming up with an original route though would be far from easy. It seemed that wherever I went there'd be little I could say that wasn't already in the trekking companies brochures! Or was there?

Lengthy examinations of a map of the Western Alps began to reveal that there was indeed a route linking 2 fantastic locations; a route that could follow mountain trails for much of its length whilst still having bad weather alternatives; a route that would traverse 2 Swiss Cantons from the northern rim of the alps almost to the Italian border as well as showing the walker some of the best mountain scenery in Europe. It couldn't be booked as a package tour either – not yet anyway.

The route would link 2 quintessentially alpine villages and their mountains which have become very symbols of the Alps themselves. My journey would take me from Grindelwald in the Canton of Bern south to Zermatt in the Valais - from the Eiger to the Matterhorn.

As the route follows several ancient pathways through the mountains, it has doubtless been walked many times, at least in part, by villagers of Bern canton visiting relatives in the southern Valais for instance. Many sections of the route have been used as trade routes throughout history though I could find no reference to the route being done for its own sake and therein lay a good reason for me to try. Besides, though it may not be a new route in the Alps in the strictest sense of the word, I thought it would make a good chapter title.

A possible downside of trying a route of my own though was that I had no itinerary to follow like the hikers on the Haute Route or TMB so I would effectively be making it up as I went along thus giving ample opportunities for getting lost. Certain sections would be fairly obvious such as the high Sefeinenfurka heading west out of the Jungfrau Region and the Gemmi or maybe Lotschen Pass from Kandersteg to the Valais but for much of the way I would be quite literally on my own.

I had at least decided on the first and last days' walking which was a start I suppose. I figured that if I was to walk from the Eiger to the Matterhorn then I should start with the wonderful "Eiger Trail" above Grindelwald and it followed that the finish, quite predictably, would be the

"Matterhorn Trail" linking Schwarzsee with Zermatt. The bit in the middle? Well; I've not thought about that yet but I suppose I'd work it out when I get there. Hmmmm!

It had seemed like the proverbial "Good idea at the time" but once I'd told a few friends and family type people that I intended to walk from Grindelwald to Zermatt I began to think that I might actually have to do this walk instead of just talk about it – after all, it was a long way over very big hills. The fact that I normally "day hike" and am not used to the concept of having to walk somewhere else day after day, regardless of weather or how knackered one is, bore down as a weight on my mind.

Hotels it would be – the best of the internet which in my case means the cheapest I can find that are still standing. Yes – I know – the "purist" would carry a tent and cooking equipment including a (very heavy) gas bottle and sleeping bag as well as clothing, food and water. Sod that for a game of soldiers! I wanted to enjoy the walk not kill myself! Anyway – the internet came up with bargain after bargain on 2/3 star hotel bookings so why rough it?

The second big test of the route was how much would I use my ability and predisposed will to cheat? Cheating on anything resembling a physical challenge was something I'd learned at school during cross country running. This sport was one I took to, more so than Rugby which at times appeared to ignore many civilised principles such as the Geneva Convention, and so I actually put the effort in on the 5 mile runs through the woods and fields managing quite good times. I did, however, find that despite all my hard work, many of the runners who mysteriously appeared ahead of me seemed a lot less tired than I was. It turned out that simply taking short cuts was the main reason behind this but there were cases of runners hopping onto the Number 37 bus which would speed them effortlessly along a third of the course at an average speed of over 25 miles an hour – a speed I was only capable of on my bike. There was even one case of a lad, David Rogers, who came in last having spent the best part of an hour enjoying tea and biscuits aboard a canal barge – speed 5 mph – not a good choice if you're looking to win a race!

Yes, cheating was a distinct possibility so I needed to decide at what point it would be resorted to. It was clearly no good going to Switzerland with the attitude that if the weather wasn't perfect I'd just say "Oh, it's raining today, I think I'll get the bus" or "It's too hot, I'll get the train up that hill" as soon as the temperature topped 25 degrees C.

Seriously though, I'd already decided after studying the map, that the vast populated trench of the Rhone valley between the southern slopes of the Bernese Alps and the climb to Zermatt would be seen through the windows of a big yellow Post Bus. The valley floor is a main through fare between Northern and Southern Europe and is built up in many places with a motorway, high speed rail links to Italy and several other roads running its length. The other places where I would allow mechanical assistance would be if there was any excessive road walking or if the path simply followed the railway lines. The purist carrying the world on his back would of course wish to walk every inch of the route but the Alpine transports, the cableways, mountain trains and Post Bus are – certainly in Switzerland – an integral part of the Alpine experience and are there to be used if required.

Chapter Two
From Blackburn to the Bernese Oberland.

How often do you actually welcome seeing the ticket inspector on a train? For most people it's probably no odds either way. For some, such as this guy I used to work with, it meant a thoroughly bad start to the day. He used to travel by train to work ticket less, having worked out the odds against being caught and when he was, he suffered not only the wrath of the inspectors but the laughter of the rest of us who thought he was a complete idiot regardless.

What this unassuming Swiss railway official was completely unaware of though was he'd just confirmed to me two very important things. Firstly, that I hadn't yet lost the ticket I'd purchased at Basel twenty minutes ago which was good going, as losing things especially small bits of paper is something of a speciality of mine, and secondly, that I was on the right train. This second point I was fairly sure of anyway but being certain is always better than being "fairly sure"!

A very un-alpine landscape, the rolling green fields and scattered towns of Northern Switzerland slid past the window as I relaxed and thought about what had been and still was, come to think of it, a very long day. Jacqui had dropped me off at Mum and Dad's house last night so as to avoid driving from Blackburn to Liverpool airport in the rush hour. As they lived abut halfway between Liverpool and Manchester airports Dad was forever getting roped in as a free airport taxi service, not only by me but by my sister as well.

Aboard Easyjet flight 7241 I had enjoyed a certain smug satisfaction that came with only having paid £7.95 for my seat. Often the day on which I go on a trip or holiday is decided by the pricing policy of Easyjet or Ryanair and this had been good one. The flight itself was uneventful and on time and it wasn't long before I was enjoying a surprisingly good slice of pizza from a station kiosk at Basel.

My train took me across Switzerland via the capital Berne which I'd visited the summer before with Jacqui and my son Josh, and a little under 2 hours after leaving Basel we were rolling along the serene shores of the Thunersee. The waters of the lake were dark beneath a grey evening sky while on the other side of the train the huge pyramid of the peak known as Niesen rose into the clouds.

The weather was surprisingly cool at Interlaken and it had clearly just been raining. The platform could have been any station in Japan judging by the main nationality of people milling around. The Japanese all seem to head for here and to Zermatt too, where I was headed. It seemed a long way off, probably because it was, and I was daunted by the prospect of walking there. For now though I'd get on a BOB train, the little red and white Berner Oberland Bahn that would take me to Grindelwald just up the valley.

Judging by the river, a huge amount of rain had fallen around here recently. There was no lazy meandering; instead a purposeful rushing marked the water's journey down valley. Above through the dripping trees, forested slopes rose at improbable angles with silvery ribbon-like waterfalls marking narrow gaps through the near vertical woods. Higher still cliffs and airy pinnacles rose into the swirling grey cloud. I've been here several times but these views never cease to amaze.

The train had reached its destination and I had begun the walk up the familiar main street of Grindelwald. Despite the crowds of people it is a charming place and it's hard to imagine anywhere more typically Swiss or Alpine. The timber chalet style shops and restaurants lined the single main street up the hill from the station, their balconies adorned with flower baskets adding splashes of colour to the scene. At this hour most of the shops selling such things as cowbell windchimes, chocolate boxes, watches and cuckoo clocks were closed and evening diners crowded onto the restaurant terraces despite the coolness of the air. There appeared to be some sort of carnival going on and walking further up the road revealed this to be, of all things, a country and western music festival. This certainly had the Japanese confused. They'd come to a place with a name like Grindelwald expecting alpine horns and lederhosen to be faced with a load of people dressed in cowboy outfits playing guitars and banjos! Some would go back to Tokyo and Osaka thinking this was what they normally did in Switzerland while others wore expressions that simply said "maybe I got on the wrong train back there".

    Resisting the temptation to stop for a beer, I walked on up the hill leaving the bustle and activity behind and headed for my hotel. Passing the church, the hill steepened and I was reminded that when I'd checked in to my flight that morning my rucksack had weighed 25 pounds. I'd packed everything I needed into a single bag, trying to keep weight to a minimum but I noticed it going up this hill. I then gradually became aware of something else; the vast scale of this valley. The high mountains hid behind the grey clouds but once away from the town centre I could sense them, towering unseen to the sky all around. Grindelwald is completely dominated by the Eiger and its North wall, the peak rising 3000 metres or 10 000 feet above the village which itself is 1000 metres above sea level. At night the lights at the Eigerwand station on the Jungfrau railway and the Mitteleggi hut on the ridge of the same name appear as stars in the black sky above, but not tonight.

    As I reached my hotel the rain began to come down again as darkness descended. I'd got here just in time. With a sense of déjà vu, I walked into the lobby of the Hotel Lauberhorn, I'd stayed here last September for a few days and I now got a warm welcome from Benny who runs the place with his wife Conny. He'd remembered my name from the booking and recognised me as I arrived.

Not wishing to carry my rucksack up to the top floor, I took the lift. Yeah, this boded well for carrying the same bag, plus food and water, across the mountains in a couple of days! The rooms at the Lauberhorn are bright and comfortable and I soon settled in, sorting my gear into what I wanted tomorrow and stuff I wouldn't have to carry until I left. I planned to do a walk the next day up a local peak. Which one depended on the weather – the rain was falling steadily and it was none too warm on the balcony. I made sure I only put in my bag things I'd need for a day hike. Having inadvertently carried a map of Snowdon up most of the hills in the Lake District and taking Wainwright's guide to the Southern Fells to Norway, I thought it was worth having a good clearout of my rucksack. I didn't need to climb 1200 metres the next day only to discover that I'd carried my guides to Zermatt and a spare pair of trainers up there as well.

I quickly showered and changed and went down to the bar for a couple of beers. Benny informed me that the forecast was improving but it hadn't been so good, wet down in Grindelwald and a lot of snow higher up – above about 2100 metres. A hiker on the Faulhorn, which I'd climbed last September, had encountered over 60cm of fresh snow 2 days previously. The Schwarzhorn was out for tomorrow as ice would render its steep rocky slopes hazardous. The slightly higher but easier Schilthorn at nearly 3000 metres would be a challenge but at least safer.

More tales of battles with the weather were recounted later when an Australian couple, Anthony and Nicky joined us. They were hiking the Oberland Pass Route which began in Engelberg. Yesterday, they'd walked over the Grosse Scheidegg from Meiringen in continuous rain and fog and were having a rest day after their ordeal. It sounded a good walk that they were doing but the weather hadn't been kind. They were doing the trek as a self guided tour which meant that they'd booked the accommodation through the tour company and it was up to them the route or mode of transport they took each day. Pretty much what I was doing really though I'd arranged my own accommodation. As a relaxing evening brought to an end a long days travelling, I headed back to my room, bravely tackling the stairs now I was without a bag.

    July 12th dawned clear and the first thing I could see when I woke up was the Eiger across the valley through the patio windows to the balcony. A towering mass of snow and ice covered rock shone in the early morning sun. Outside were revealed all the peaks that had been invisible the previous night - across the valley the Eiger and the Fiescherhorner, while at the end of the valley rose the equally precipitous Wetterhorn. Glaciers draped low towards the valley and the snowline, also hidden last night, was much lower than normal for July, a winter world only 1000 m above.

    After an excellent breakfast I wandered leisurely back down the road to the railway station and bought my ticket to Murren, an experience made so much more enjoyable by using the half-price card I'd bought in Basel. These cards, known as *halbtax* in German and *demi tarif* in French speaking Switzerland, are valid for a month and cost about £35. They enable the purchaser to travel half price on all Swiss National and Regional railways as well as the Post Bus service and most of the non-state run trains and cable cars, including the Jungfraubahn and the BOB trains operating in this region. They're even valid on most boat services on the lakes throughout the country. It always pleased me to get anything half price anyway.

The cowboys had left town and the shops in Grindelwald were back to normal selling cuckoo clocks and cow-bell wind chimes. My mum had bought some once and they'd hung on the back door until the noise kept everyone awake at night and they were taken down. My train journey took me back down the valley to change at Zwei Lutschinen where I boarded another to Lauterbrunnen a short way to the south. (Staying on the first train would have taken me back down to Interlaken.) The weather here was a shade warmer but cloud was beginning to gather around the peaks obscuring many of them from view.

I boarded the cable car for Grutschalp which had replaced the old funicular. I decided this would be one I'd use on the walk when I passed through Lauterbrunnen in 2 days time. It doesn't cut out much distance just a steep climb on a path linking the top and bottom stations. From Grutschalp a second train takes you along a wide forested shelf into Murren. This place was surprisingly quiet after the busy streets of Grindelwald and Lauterbrunnen and only a few tourists wandered onto its streets. I passed the hotel

Jungfrau – Good – I was booked in there in 3 night's time and it looked a pleasant chalet building on a quiet road. I took the short funicular railway to Almendhubel which knocks an hour or so off the lengthy climb to the Schilthorn.

Surrounded by the lifting mists which had hung just above Murren I began the ascent. Almendhubel is situated in an area of cool damp woods and grassy alpine meadows at an altitude of about 1900 m and the path (signposted Schilthorn and Schilthorn hut) led up from the station to a small summit where an information board gave facts abut the Eiger which was hidden somewhere in the mist behind me.

The path led downhill slightly at first along a wide grassy ridge before beginning a steep and unrelenting ascent of the slope ahead. This is the course of the Inferno Ski Run from the Schilthorn's summit down to Murren. Looking at the gradient it would appear that only a grisly death on the rocks below could result from skiing down here. Equally mad, a sign declared it to be the route of a half marathon! I'll not be entering either race.

It was a peaceful rest stop. Silence apart from distant cowbells and the sound of an unseen stream somewhere. As I watched, the eternal snows of the Jungfrau emerged half seen across the valley. The contrast of the sunlit snow and dark rock hung like a mirage in a hole in the clouds before fading away as the mist closed back in.

All of a sudden, the path turned a sharp left up a wide gully before the angle at last eased and the country opened out. I walked for some time over cropped turf of alpine meadows climbing slowly but steadily. The mist surrounded everything but it didn't rain and the path was clear to follow. Presently I started to spot patches of melting snow which became more frequent until ahead a seemingly endless snow slope emerged from the drifting cloud.

A group of hikers, who turned out to be English, took form from the fog and informed me that the hut wasn't far, "just 5 minutes". They'd taken the cable car to Birg at 2600m and walked down. The way at least that far was easy despite the snow, but they didn't know what the route to the summit was like.

Up the snow I went and indeed reached a sign in a couple of minutes pointing to the hut just off to the left. From here the way was barred – apparently a rock fall had come down and made the main path hazardous. I followed the diversion to the left across more snow and all of a sudden a gap in the cloud opened up. The way ahead was seen up the snowfields in the middle.

Another steep haul, kicking steps in the snow as I followed the new route up through a remote looking high valley brought me back to the main path and the going at once became easier again. Here were 2 more walkers up ahead. I must say for a mountain that is accessible by cable car, I'd seen surprisingly few people. Maybe it was the weather or amount of snow but I'd have expected more walking downhill if not climbing the peak. They turned out to be an American couple who'd also walked down from

Birg, the middle station, which had been visible above as I climbed the valley.

"It's just great to be without the car", commented the guy, "not having to worry about parking and finding gas". I agreed and told them that I never bothered with one in Switzerland – you don't need a car here, the transport is so good; totally different from being in the States, where buses and trains are few and far between away from the cities. I guess Britain's about half way between the two.

We bade each other well for the rest of our walks and I headed on up, following a sign for the Schilthorn again. The main path led off around the slope to the left for Birg but my route kept on up to the ridge between the 2 peaks. I guessed it was unusual to find an American who disliked cars, but I just had.

My route now led past a mountain tarn below to the left, with the cloud revealing a variable amount of the snowy wilderness I headed into. Down beyond the tarn there were occasional glimpses of the Lauterbrunnen valley through the ragged clouds. It was a long, long way down and I was surprised how high I was. The air here was thin and cold and the snow was no longer melting. For a while the Jungfrau was visible again and there was blue sky as if I was emerging above the cloud but as I climbed the mist overtook me again.

The route was marked by red and white splotches of paint and small cairns here and there, so despite the snow cover, now 6 or more inches deep in places, the way was easy to find. Up and over rocks in short scrambles followed by plods through deep snow. I paused by a rock as I needed the loo, first listening out to see if the cable car was near by. I didn't want to be caught with my pants down just as the cable car appeared out of the mist, its full load of tourists clicking away on their cameras. The thought of the cable car appearing amused me, it didn't of course – I'd gone under its path some way back. I presently passed a memorial to Alice Arbuthnot who was killed up here by lightning in 1865. This served to remind me of the dangers and concentrate on the job in hand.

As the path steepened great care was needed on the snowy parts but soon sections of fixed rope appeared as the route began to follow the crest of the ridge. Beyond it was a misty white void. I reached a minor summit just as the sun came out. Beyond, the fixed rope led across a narrow section of ridge only a foot or two wide, the summit just beyond, with the famous restaurant clearly visible on top.

I set off across the narrow section, it was a bit like Sharp Edge in the Lake District but the proximity of the cloud tops gave the sensation of walking in the sky. Just to add to the impression of height – as if it needed to – holes in the cloud revealed the Lauterbrunnen valley over 2000m below while snow peaks floated dizzily on the fog banks like some great oceanic icebergs on its far side. Below the cloud closer at hand was revealed a mysterious high valley with no sign of habitation which disappeared back beneath the cloud layers before I could identify it.

I was soon, with some help from the rope handrail, across this rather exciting section and climbing the rocks on the far side by a series of stone steps hewn out of the rock itself. A last breathless climb brought me onto the summit structure where people milled about looking cold and somewhat the worse for the altitude. The Schilthorn is 2970m or nearly 10 000 feet so a rapid ascent from valley level on the cable car would quite literally take your breath away.

The views from here are famous and extend from the Black Forest in Germany to Mont Blanc but today they didn't! We appeared to be level with the top of the cloud layer so sometimes the sun shone and some of the nearer mountains were visible then the mist would roll back over us hiding all but this cold airy platform.

I went inside for a minute but it was too warm and crowded so I amused myself by watching the tourists come dashing out for a view of the Eiger only for the cloud to come back in before they could get their cameras out of their bags. The simple things are always the best! Besides, it had happened to me already several times. Apparently there's a cinema up here where you can watch James Bond in *On Her Majesty's Secret Service* which was partly filmed here. They still mention this in the tourist blurb even though it was a good few years ago now. I've seen the film, so I didn't bother.

Because of the time I opted against retracing my steps down, instead taking the easy option of a one way ticket in the cable car - half price of course - at least retaining an element of smugness with the knowledge that out of the population of that dangling metal box I was the only one to have actually climbed the mountain.

Feeling that healthy tiredness that only comes from a long day's outdoor exertion I made my way back up Grindelwald's main street in search of food. In fact I wasn't really searching; I knew exactly where I was headed. At the top end of the village there's a small restaurant by the roadside called *Tom's Hutte* and they do an excellent pizza – one of the best in fact and ten minutes later I was sat outside that very restaurant, a beer on the table, awaiting a spicy chilli pizza.

The pizza lived up to usual standards and still feeling a warm fatigue but no longer hungry I went back to my hotel before I fell asleep outside the restaurant. There was no sign of the Aussies, Anthony and Nicky that night, but I only went in the bar for a short while before heading to my room.

Tomorrow was Friday the 13th. It was also the day I would set off on my first proper trek in the Alps across one of the most notorious mountains in the world, the Eiger. Okay I wasn't going up the North face but along the path known as the Eiger Trail that led below it but I'm not superstitious about these things so I didn't care anyway. With the weather forecast promising or threatening (depending on whether or not you had a long uphill walk to do carrying a heavy pack) 30 degrees C tomorrow an early start would be needed.

Chapter Three
Friday the 13th on the Eiger

A brilliant cloudless blue morning awaited me as I began the walk down the road from the hotel. Feeling fortified from a good breakfast I'd checked out of the Lauberhorn and begun my journey. The Oberland Mountains shone in the clear air and beckoned me on my way – not too quickly though - my pack was a bit heavy!

By the church I turned off on a road which I thought went to Grund, the village just below Grindelwald. It didn't. I ended up following a track through the farmland below the village which eventually brought me, after half and hour, back to the village only 200m further down than where I'd left the main road. Good start!

This time on the right track, a footpath led down again past scattered houses and farms and down to the shade-less valley floor. The sun blazed down and I was already sweating despite having walked mainly downhill.

"It's too hot", I thought to myself. "I think I'll get the train up that hill." The hill I referred to was the path following the Jungfrau railway from Grund to Alpiglen, a steep climb but the Eiger Trail officially started at Alpiglen, so I guess it was only a small cheat.

It was a relief to get off the crowded train at Alpiglen and it was slightly cooler up here. I was surprised that there was no-one about and the Café looked closed but it was still early, I'd left the hotel just after 8am. Having sorted my bag into a more comfortable position I, at last, set off.

There are two main ways from Grindelwald to Kleine Scheidegg and thence to Wengen, where I was headed today; the pass known as Kleine Scheidegg, which my Aussie mates would be tackling on the Oberland Pass Route, and the Eiger Trail, which I was on now. This route I had done in a downwards direction from Eigergletcher station last year. In this direction though, you climb to Eigergletcher, then descend about 1000 feet to Kleine Scheidegg. From there the way to Wengen is the same but this route gives a closer view of the North Face of the Eiger.

The well marked path signposted the Eiger Trail, led up across an open meadow towards a patch of trees. The views here were amazing with the whole of the Grindelwald valley laid out below and the Wetterhorn at its end above the wide saddle of the Grosse Scheidegg pass. To the other side of the pass heading across the valley rose the green range of the Faulhorn topped by the shining white peak of the Schwarzhorn. The name means 'black peak' and I found it amusing that it was the only completely snow covered – hence not black at all – summit in that range.

I soon reached the trees but the still shade was no cooler. The path wound up steeply through them and across a little ledge with a rope handrail - I remembered that from the last time - before zigzagging up again above the trees.

I stopped for a rest and some water and was overtaken by a couple who seemed to be sprinting up. I'd had to stop otherwise I would have flaked out with the heat! Setting off again the trail levelled a little before I branched off to the right crossing a little footbridge where the river had channelled a mini gorge in the limestone and back towards Eigergletcher. A steep section followed – with many rests! If the breeze stopped so did I – to wait for it to start again.

A Japanese couple passed me going the other way at one of my rest stops. They spoke good English and said the forecast was for temperatures of 30 to 35 degrees centigrade in the valley over the weekend. Hang on – what's this 35 all about? I thought 30 would be the top!

It was too hot already, my bag weighed, my strength ebbed and it felt as though I was being boiled from the inside. The North Wall above was draped in huge amounts of ice and snow and its cool shadows looked inviting rather than threatening. I was sure of one thing – if this heat kept up I would not be going to Zermatt.

Higher up the path follows huge, grassy, and then stony hollows beneath the North Wall. It was more open here and the breeze returned. I realised that I needed to stop for longer, not just for a minute, and allow myself to cool down properly. The same as if your car has over-heated you need to let it fully cool down before setting off again.

Steadily, I climbed and the battle with the sun was finally won with help from the Eiger itself! There was a stretch below the wall where the path was shaded by the mountain. I made for this and stopped for a snack and water.

A sound like a series of rumbling cracks broke the stillness. Above, an avalanche of ice, snow and rock was crashing down the fearsome crags. The face, first climbed in July 1938 by Heinrich Harrer, Anderl Heckmair, Ludwig Vorg and Fritz Kasparek, has a reputation for notoriety. Harrer's brilliant book *The White Spider* recounts the full history of climbing the face as well as the deaths, narrow escapes and heroic rescue attempts that have resulted from attempting it. The names of many of its features; the Hinterstossier Traverse, Death Bivouac, Traverse of the Gods and the White Spider itself evoke tales of bravery and tragedy. Yet despite the very real dangers of climbing this King of Alpine North Faces, the Eiger has killed far fewer climbers than say, Mont Blanc whose normal route can be hazardous too, but is not particularly difficult in good conditions.

I think though that to attempt the Eiger North Face, one would need to be part of a special breed of climbers. If you weren't of the calibre needed you'd know it and wouldn't risk the attempt. Many try Mont Blanc mistakenly thinking it to be an easy walk up. It isn't. Many don't come back.

Another avalanche broke my reverie and I decided against attempting to climb the 1800 metres of sheer, ice-encrusted, crumbling limestone above me and instead see if I could get up this footpath. I watched as the avalanche became a fine white dust cloud hanging in the air and set off once again.

I was almost chilly after resting in some proper shade and could now walk at a decent pace without stopping every two minutes. Up a short steep section and into the last stony hollow, I passed the sprinters from before; they were now resting by the path. Soon afterwards I passed an area of small cairns I remembered from last time - I think they are memorials to dead climbers but don't quote me on that – I'm not certain.

This really is a good path. It was constructed but not with big stone steps or - even worse - concrete, as some paths are. It's narrow, easy and obvious and follows a fantastic route. I was feeling good again in the cool breeze at 2300m – I was going to Zermatt after all!

The last section leads below the sheer rock outcrop of the Rotstock, a small subsidiary peak of the Eiger and you walk on a shady, narrow section below the rock wall and then, all of a sudden, there are open meadows and a view of the Monch and Jungfrau – Eigergletcher, 7,650 feet.

I walked up the ridge, past where the original Mittellegi Hut has been relocated and up to a seat in the shade below the overhanging rocks. A good lunch spot – it was where I'd nearly been blown off the ridge last September. Today was calm though and a man sunbathed on the south side of the ridge. His dog had more sense and wandered up to join me in the shade.

It was a good lunchtime perch with views close up on the Monch and Jungfrau and their glaciers. Ahead and below, a long way below, was the Lauterbrunnen valley, and beyond that the snow topped Schilthorn that I'd climbed yesterday.

After a look around the corner where a faint path led along a ledge and up towards the Rotstock via ferrata, a rock route on the ridge protected by fixed ropes and ladders, I nipped into the Eigergletcher station for an orange juice on the terrace. I'd eaten here last time and the food had been good.

Many open air restaurants in the Alps have a population of opportunistic birds – usually sparrows - which will virtually join you at the table in the hope of a few scraps. Here at Eigergletcher though, perhaps in keeping with the Eiger's reputation, there sat on the fence several great black ravens, like so many extras from a Hitchcock movie!

Downhill now - an easy path headed down towards Kleine Scheidegg and, just before the station, traversed a particularly horrible building site. What an achievement! They'd succeeded in destroying, not only the peace and quiet, but also quite a large area of alpine meadow land and created an eyesore. I hope they're proud of themselves.

I carried on to Kleine Scheidegg, where I'd planned a short stop, but today in the sunshine, it was even more crowded than usual, so I just carried on. The track was good and the views breathtaking but the heat returned as I dropped lower and while I'd left the crowds of the Scheidegg behind it was still busy. Just as I was becoming bored with walking with all the tourists, many of whom looked the type that would never have got up here without the train and were only capable of walking if it was downhill, I was distracted by a large bird circling over the Jungfrau's crags, riding thermals of warm air. I was fairly sure I'd just seen an eagle but the distance was too great to be certain.

At the Wengernalp, where I stopped for a cold drink, I overheard an English voice behind me saying that he'd spotted a golden eagle half an hour previously. They sounded as though they knew more about bird watching than I did, which isn't very much, so that will do for me, it *was* an eagle I'd just seen.

The proprietor of the Wengernalp, who served me, spoke English and he asked how far I was going.

"To Zermatt", I'd replied. He'd seemed very interested in my quest when I elaborated on my planned route and as I was leaving he came over again and gave me a large piece of cake.

"On the house", he said. "For the Sefeinenfurka – just in case – there's nothing up there!"

I thanked the man profusely – I always like getting something for free, but it was a kind act and I appreciated it. I would indeed save it for lunch on the Sefeinenfurka.

Here I was joined, for a while, by Ben from Boston who'd overheard me talking about my trip. He'd not done so badly. A long flight to Geneva that morning, followed by a drive to Interlaken and the Mannlichen cable car which he'd walked down from just now on his way back to Wengen.

Soon the first views down to Wengen appeared and on down towards Interlaken beyond. I was on a sunny meadow just above the tree line and some guys were getting ready to paraglide down. I nearly asked them for a lift. I was hot again and it was a relief to be back in the trees for a long, lonely walk on an endless forest path.

Emerging from the cool pines into the sun again I heard the sound of cow bells close at hand. Just to the right was a field of donkeys. Yes, donkeys – all wearing cow bells or would they be called donkey bells? Either that or the sun had got to my head and I was hallucinating them! How surreal.

Tired out, I arrived in Wengen and began the search for the Hotel Belvedere, where I was booked in that night. My walk had been good so far though the weather had made it a lot harder and now all I wanted was a sit down, a shower, a beer and food, in that order.

Wengen, like Grindelwald, is another typical Swiss alpine village, charming and excessively pretty, it exudes an opulent exclusivity and I was lucky I think to have found a room with breakfast for 80 francs or just over £30. Many will know Wengen from programmes like the U.K.'s Ski Sunday, it being home to the famous Lauberhorn Downhill race and the railway station has a board displaying the names of the heroes of this race headed by American star Bodie Miller.

As I walked slowly up the road towards my hotel – Swiss villages usually have signposts to individual hotels – I realised what added to the peaceful atmosphere here. Like Zermatt, where I was headed, Wengen is traffic free, the only transport being the electric buggies which can be just as lethal as you can't hear them coming up behind you. I didn't however miss the pollution and noise of cars. The week before, Jacqui, Josh and I had been to London to watch the start of the Tour de France and the difference it made when the roads were closed for the race was unbelievable. One could actually appreciate the city's wonderful architecture and tree lined roads in peace, quiet and clean air.

It is ominous when a hotel receptionist says any sentence containing the words "a problem with your booking". Here at the Belvedere a trade delegation of some description had apparently booked the whole hotel leaving me and several other guests out in the cold as it were. So much for my making comments about Friday 13th! While not wishing to share with a bunch of pompous business people I did require a lie down within the next half hour or so.

The receptionist however, soon had me reassured. "You'll be stopping at our sister hotel the Wengener Hof next door." I was further reassured on being told that I would still have breakfast and it would not cost one penny more.

This was landing on one's feet! The red carpet and 4 stars painted on the door promised a splendour that I was unaccustomed to! The Belvedere had looked nice – old style and friendly but the Wengener Hof was the lap of luxury.

My room was about the size of Luxembourg and even the shower compartment was as big as our bathroom at home. I immediately lowered the tone of the place by washing socks and shirts and hanging them on the balcony to dry.

The restaurant was one of those where people dressed for dinner and it looked expensive so I headed off in search of somewhere cheap and preferably Italian. A little bar/restaurant about 100m from the hotel answered all requirements and I enjoyed a delicious seafood risotto outdoors in the now pleasantly warm evening.

As I was finishing my meal and on my second or third beer, my attention was caught by a group of English tourists at a neighbouring table as the waitress brought them a bottle of wine which was clearly neither their first nor second for that matter.

One woman was educating the others on the art of cooking salmon and after a lengthy talk on the subject she declared that she wasn't very big on salmon in the first place. Another piped up with "No, not on its own, it's got to have something on it."

"I prefer a nice bit of trout" added a third lady, who sounded as though she would lose the ability to speak if she drank any more wine.

A slurred and sonorous male voice then brought the subject of halibut into the conversation. Well, that was it. Halibut would keep them going all night as each member of the group reminisced with eloquence about their own personal experiences of that particular fish.

I was sorely tempted to add my own comments about a fish licence for a pet 'alibut, referring to a sketch by Monty Python but couldn't remember the lines. It was time to go!

A bottle of beer from the minibar and I sat out on the balcony and took photos of the surrounding mountains. The sun was setting and the alpenglow lit the Jungfrau and Breithorn splendidly. My position, with the flower boxes on the balcony, backed by a lush line of trees and the green carpet of the valley floor far below gave the impression of being in a vast hanging garden. As the lights began to appear one by one in the valley, the only sounds were evening birdsong and the ever present distant cow bells – or were they donkeys? One never knows!

Chapter Four
Smoked Salmon for Breakfast

Before I came to the Alps for this trip I had never envisaged having smoked salmon for breakfast, it just somehow hadn't entered my plans. Breakfast at the Wengener Hof was a thoroughly good start to the day.

Relieving the room of a variety of shampoos, shower gels and soaps, I checked out and shouldered my bag.

"Would you like your bag taking to the station sir?" enquired the concierge.

"Er, no thanks, I'm O.K", I replied. If I couldn't carry my own bag to the station I didn't fancy my chances crossing the Sefeinenfurka the next day.

The weather was already hot and I was glad I'd decided to have a short day. I'd take the train and cable car to Grutchalp which was less than 2 miles away directly across the Lauterbrunnen valley, before travelling an easy but scenic section from there to Murren. I stopped briefly to have a look at a small white church near the hotel which overlooked the valley from the edge of Wengen before heading down to the station.

Lauterbrunnen in its sheltered trench like valley was tropically hot and crowded. Wengen had been busy but this place was noisy too. It has the motor road as well as the railway station side by side and everyone seemed to get off here whether they were coming here or not. People would leave their train carriage and wander around the platform for a while, perhaps going in the café before getting into another carriage, though a few would quite inexplicably get back on the same train.

I followed the signs that said 'Murren' and 'Grutchalp' and was led to the Grutchalp cable car. This replaced the funicular that used to operate here and I'm sure it can shift even more tourists per hour! It was definitely busier than a couple of days before when I'd been here to go up the Schilthorn. What appeared to be hundreds of suitcases of varying shapes and sizes were loaded onto a platform beneath the cable car, presumably destined for the hotels of traffic free Murren. I bravely carried my own bag all by myself and without the assistance of a fork lift truck all the way up the dozen or so steps the board the cable car.

It was 24 degrees centigrade at Grutchalp despite its altitude of nearly 1500m. It was however, more comfortable than the valley. Looking back I could just make out the church and my hotel slightly below and on the opposite side. It was definitely too warm though to have walked up from Lauterbrunnen.

I set off along a wide path which passed through numerous pleasant shady patches beneath tall pine trees, taking a slow, steady pace to avoid getting too warm. The lack of breeze, I think, caused more discomfort than the actual temperature. Presently, I crossed the stream of the Staubbach by a small footbridge. Just below here it plunges into space over the vast cliff dominating Lautbrunnen to form the spectacular Staubbach Falls which many of Lauterbrunnen's tourists had come to look at. Here, though, it was just another stream emerging from the woods.

This path really was easy. Kids in buggies were being pushed along in places though, perhaps surprisingly, it wasn't that busy. Ever present between the trees were the great white peaks of the Eiger, Monch and Jungfrau on the left while ahead rose the snowy Ebneflue which, along with the Monch, is one of the easier high summits around here. Despite the very easy angle of the path, the sun soon had me wanting to stop for a cold drink and this I did at Winteregg.

"*Ein orangensaft mit eis bitte?*" I enquired of the waiter here, resisting the temptation to have a beer – it WAS too early! This was becoming a much used and very useful German phrase as it got me a glass of fresh orange full of ice cubes. These places are fantastic. On most popular Alpine trails you can usually find a mountain inn or *berghaus* along the way which will provide food and drink and in many cases accommodation as well.

From Winteregg there was a short climb up through trees before the path became almost level following the railway line into Murren. I was glad I'd walked the bulk of the distance instead of riding the train all the way and was overcome by a feeling of intense smugness as a trainload of tourists passed me. Hah – they couldn't even be bothered to walk that nice easy bit with those wonderful views. The final section into Murren though was in the sun and sheltered from any breeze whatsoever so when the route became a tarmac road with a concrete wall to one side, I was strongly reminded of one of those clay ovens that they cook kebabs in.

I easily find the Hotel Jungfrau – probably because I'd seen it the other day – and am soon enjoying a hot shower in a bathroom which appears to be lit by a 5 watt bulb. So dark is this bathroom with or without the light on that I nearly resorted to my head torch to see the shower controls. Not to worry, I feel much better for the shower and am soon relaxed on the bed watching the Tour de France on T.V. The room may be small compared to the vast acreage of last night's room, but it is comfortable.

I find it strange watching the peleton approaching the Alps. At home whenever they get to the Alps or the Pyrenees I'm always wishing I was there and now I am, surrounded by even better scenery than the cyclists and spectators are. The stage is won by a German rider, Gerdemann. That must be so fantastic - approaching the stage finish and looking behind to see no-one in pursuit.

The manager and receptionist very kindly reserve me a room at tomorrow's destination, Griesalp, in the Kiental, away across the mountain. They thought I'd better be on the safe side as it was the summer holidays and there are only about two hotels there.

Tea is spaghetti Bolognese on the terrace at the rear of the hotel. It's an area of wooden decking looking onto a meadow sloping steeply up to a line of pines which is just the kind of place you'd expect Julie Andrews to come running down in full song but instead cows begin to appear one by one from the forest. Their presence seemed out of place and I watched them absently.

I really will have to have something other than pasta or pizza while I am here. It's just that they're tasty and cheap. The local German style dishes are fine – *Schnitzel* – a kind of breaded pork steak; *rosti* – fried grated potato; or the various sausages on offer are all good. I don't suffer from the same restaurant paranoia as I do in France about being given something cooked in a cream sauce (which I don't like) or undercooked meat (which will make me throw up), though the dire shortage of curry houses in both countries is a major culinary problem. Oh for a chicken bhuna!

That evening I wander around Murren for a while amazed at how quiet the streets are. Where are the owners of all those suitcases that the cable car brought up here? Murren is made up of the same wooden chalet style hotels and tourist oriented shops as Grindelwald and Wengen but there's hardly a soul about. I walk down towards the station and back along the road below my hotel which leads to the end of the village and the path up the mountains where I will be heading tomorrow. I wander back to the hotel for a beer where the manager asks me about my walk. He seems very impressed with the route I was doing – as has been everyone who I've told so far. Maybe I'm taking on too much here and it will be tougher than I thought.

I speak to Jacqui on the phone and she tells me that it's raining back home and they had to put the fire on at her Mum and Dad's house in Cumbria where she was for the weekend. I just wish it were cool enough to need a fire I say but she's unsympathetic – funny that.

Tomorrow would be the first big test; across the mountains to Kiental. There were no trains or buses up there, the only form of transport was the boot and it was a long way, everyone had said that. Even so it was the first wilderness region I was passing through and one I was looking forward to. It would be very different to the tourist areas I had seen so far on the trip.

As I write this, all the cows seem to have found their way out from the trees and returned to their nocturnal habitat of the meadow. Quite why they were in the forest in the first place I'm not sure but I guess they too had had enough of the sun.

Chapter Five
Into the Wilds

Breakfast was from 7am so being ready and downstairs for 6.55 am; I thought I'd have the place to myself. Not to be – a large party of Japanese walkers were already there and when the order was given they started a military style operation to clear the buffet tables. I managed to get my share though and retired to the lonely stance that is the curse of the single traveller – the table for one.

If the restaurant is quiet I don't unduly notice that I'm eating on my own but one's lack of table companions is somewhat heightened at busy times, when everyone else is chatting away. I felt like Billy No Mates with a contagious disease!

Their leader stood up after she had decided everyone had eaten enough. Clearly enjoying herself, she barked a couple more orders and the place cleared as quickly as it had filled. Strange customs the Japanese, I'll say one thing though – they never cause any trouble and always have a smile for you even when they don't speak English.

On the road before 8 am – it's not often I can say that! I crossed the bridge I'd visited last night and began walking up the road beyond. It's normally cool at this hour but not today. As the scattered houses of Murren dropped slowly below and behind me it was airless. I walked slowly up past hay meadows and pastures to the sound of crickets by the roadside. It was amazingly peaceful up here beyond the village, and the mountains rose into the still air far above the valley which remained in dawn twilight below.

As the sun gathered strength the harder it became and sweat poured down my face stinging my eyes and I seemed to fight gravity every inch of the way.

Presently I left the road, following the signed track through pastures and came to a little berghaus called Spielbodenalp. Here I sat in the shade and drank orange juice before having another go. This promised to be another day of solar onslaught as I tackled the steep path above Spielbodenalp.

This section with breathtaking views back to the Jungfrau and Eiger and far down to the valley somewhere near Stechelberg would normally be an exhilarating walk. The path wound steadily up, spiralling towards a high limestone outcrop edging out onto the cliffs themselves in its upper sections.

I was going at my limit, maybe 2 miles an hour. My head pounded and my bag felt as though it contained a baby elephant. Looking at the rocks in front there appeared a great number of lizards. They became more numerous and mesmerising and their movement was punctuated at intervals by regular bright flashes of light. I stopped to see where they came from and they faded into the rocks, thought he flashes continued. Looking round the world seemed distant as through a tunnel and there was a sound like the ocean. I tried to move and couldn't, so half sat and half fell down instead. I don't know how long later – I think only about 10 minutes – I felt slightly more normal and drank most of my water.

I was reminded of the tragic tale of Tommy Simpson, one of Britain's best ever professional cyclists who collapsed and died of exhaustion on Mont Ventoux in conditions probably very like these. Like me, Tommy had chosen to do what he did though the big difference between us was that he wasn't content just to finish on the Ventoux – he HAD to win. I didn't need to win anything. All I had to do was finish and just now I nearly hadn't.

The immediate concern was to get to shade or at least off this south facing sun trap.

I toyed with the idea of going back down but quickly decided against this. I knew I could do it; the problem was I can cope with most conditions apart from these. I drank the rest of my water, knowing the hut wasn't a vast distance away and slowly climbed the last of the steep slope to reach a more level path contouring the slopes above. This trail crossed a wide, steep, grassy mountainside with some stunning views but I really can't remember their detail. The going was easier but I was constantly reminded of a movie I'd seem years before during which some desert explorers or plane crash survivors, I'm not sure now which they were, had to cross a particularly hot and waterless region called 'The Sun's Anvil'. I still can't remember the title of the movie.

In true seventies movie fashion, I was served lunch and a huge bottle of fizzy water by a particularly attractive blonde girl who spoke good English at the Rotstockhutte. The hut lies in the valley below the Schilthorn at a height of 2039 metres and is the last place for refreshments before Griesalp in the next valley, the Kiental.

The girl told me that the week before there had been snow here and over 40cm at the pass. She also said that in the bad weather – rain and snow – nearly all the walkers who visit the hut seem to be English. I reply that it's because rain's the norm to us. If we won't go walking in the Lakes or Scotland when it's wet, then we'll hardly ever go walking.

I add that I'd prefer the snow to this heat any day and she reassures that, though today and yesterday have been around 35 degrees C in the valley, it was cooling down from now on.

"Gooday! How's it going mate?" Now, there's a familiar voice. It was Anthony and Nicky, who'd been staying at the Lauberhorn in Grindelwald. They joined me for lunch and we compared notes on our journeys here. That was, after we'd moved round the corner out of sight of the sign that said 'No Picnics' so they could eat their packed lunch instead of buying anything.

They'd walked to Wengen via the Kleine Scheidegg the day I'd done the Eiger Trail and Anthony described the path as being great until you actually reach Kleine Scheidegg.

They'd tramped over a hill from the peace and quiet of the trail to be faced with the crowds and general awfulness of Kleine Scheidegg. Like me they'd walked straight through and stopped at Wengenalp instead. The day before they'd had a rest day and taken the train all the way from Wengen to Murren and had actually seen me – looking very hot apparently – walking towards Murren weighed down by my rucksack. I hadn't seen them but maybe they were on the train that passed me on the last stretch. The smug feeling I'd experienced returned once more.

It was good to see familiar faces and catch up on experiences but soon it was time to be off once more and I left them to openly flout the no picnics rule and saying I'd no doubt see them later as I planned to take it very slowly from here.

Beyond the hut is a wonderful landscape of green pastures and silver streams. Above on one side rose the grey cliffs of the Schilthorn with very little snow left on this south facing side. I realised that this was the mysterious high valley I'd spotted through the clouds from near the narrow ridge. Behind lay the snow capped summits surrounding the head of the Lauterbrunnen valley and ahead was my route. The path made a steep ascent of the slopes to the right of a prominent rock face.

It was cooler here but I still took it slowly uphill and stopped for several rests until the angle eased and the path followed a wide valley up behind the rock peak below a long slope of scree and snow patches which rose to the left. Here Anthony and Nicky, together with an English guy doing the same walk - whose name I never did get - caught me up but I said I'd see them at the top as I was determined not to overdo it again.

The track soon crossed a snowfield and began to steepen up a slope of dark shaly rock. The crest of the Sefeinenfurka which marked the end of the area known as the *Jungfrau Region* was a jagged ridge not far above. Soon I was about level with the summit of Birg by the Schilthorn across the valley and, going better in the cool air at 2600m, I now climbed the last steep, loose slope to the rocky summit of the pass.

The Sefeinenfurka, at 2612m, is a great mountain pass in every sense of the word. A narrow saddle with steep slopes - precipitous even - dropping off on both sides. The far side was steeper than the one I'd just come up and from that side the pass was a notch in a wall of cliffs. Behind me the Eiger, Monch and Jungfrau, now looking distant, rose across the unseen depths of the Lauterbrunnen valley, whilst, in what was now the far distance, the still - white top of the Schwarzhorn was visible. That was near to where I'd started. It looked a long way and I felt a sense of achievement.

Ahead was a totally new landscape of unfamiliar sharp rocky peaks with the only area of snow being the Bluemlisalp further along on the ridge. Below the ground fell almost vertically to a wild valley with no signs of human habitation and in the blue distance were lower green and wooded mountains while beyond them was the haze over the lowlands. I really had a profound sense of leaving one region and entering another.

"Who says there's no such thing as a free lunch" I commented as I ate my free almond cake given to me at the Wengenalp. It tasted all the better for being free and the guy had been right. There was nothing up here.

It was with some trepidation that we set off one by one down the far side of the pass. The route followed a precipitous loose slope on wooden steps with a fixed rope to hang on to. They were awkward with a big rucksack and numbered probably seven or eight hundred, though no-one counted them. In places the cliff overhung above to the extent that you almost had to duck to get down. When the steps ended, there was loose shale to walk down; still a long way above the river and it was a relief to still have the rope.

Eventually we all made it to an area that didn't seem about to collapse into the bottom of the valley and were able to resume walking normally. The English guy had by now shot off ahead, Anthony saying that he was one of those who always wanted to be first at the hotel or bunkhouse, but the three of us stuck together.

Always downhill, the path led past some spectacular waterfalls while the craggy walls of the valley rose higher and higher as we descended. Presently we arrived at a river crossing which we took our time over almost getting into the freezing water. The weather had become hot again with our descent and it felt so good to pour the cold water over my head.

On again - always downhill. This was an amazing valley, a stony wilderness so unlike the grassy meadows above Murren. Soon we came to the first signs of habitation, empty and abandoned hay barns and then fenced pastures with cows grazing. The white Bluemlisalp towered above, while below the pinewoods of the Kiental could be now be seen framed by valley walls of alternate sloping green pasture and sheer limestone precipices.

We followed a steep path down through pastures to the first inhabited hamlets and for a short while followed a wide track, really an unsurfaced road, before branching off on a forest path disappearing down into the pines.

It was cooler in the forest and a very pleasant walk took us to Griesalp. My friends were staying at the *Golderli* chalet which we came to first. They were unsure of their plans for tomorrow apart from that they were going to Kandersteg. The Alpine pass route goes over the Hohturli pass – another long day. Their preference though was for the bus, which I must confess is looking like a favourite for me as well.

My route can go whichever way I want as I'm making it up as I go along. Certainly if it were a good deal cooler I would consider the Hohturli, being a direct route to Kandersteg, though, from the look at the map, I quite like the idea of going right off the beaten track and crossing to the next valley the Kandertal by some path marked to the north of here from Kiental over to Frutigen or along the *hohenweg* (high route) known as the *Nordramp* to Kandersteg. Either way I'd get the post bus in the morning down to

Kiental village to start one of those routes. I was determined not to get the bus the whole way to Kandersteg.

"See you on the bus in the morning" they both said as they went into the Berghaus Golderli, which looked an inviting hostelry. Seems they'd already decided on their plans.

I walked the kilometre or so to the Berghaus Griesalp a little further down the valley down a woodland path which led for its last section alongside a fast-flowing river that seemed to cool the air under the shady trees.

"How much?" I ask in disbelief. A hundred and twenty francs is around fifty quid, which makes the Hotel Griesalp the most expensive on my trip by fully 25 francs. My room is good with a vast shower compartment but I immediately look for anything detachable such as light bulbs in order to recoup a little of my investment. I then realise that anything misappropriated from the room would need to be carried all the way to Zermatt and I abandon the idea.

Tea consists of chicken and chips on a sunny terrace outside. Most of the people it seems have come up for the day, this being the end of the road served by the post bus. I notice that all the voices without exception are German. No English, American, Japanese or even French voices can be heard.

The waitress speaks to a couple opposite in an accent that sounds Norwegian and a language that must be mainly German though I distinctly heard the words; "hello", "salut" and "merci" in there several times. The customer, a middle aged man, who I presumed was German rather than

Swiss looks at his wife in puzzlement and throws up his arms and says in exasperation *Schweizer Deutsch!* If they didn't understand, how was I going to fare? I can hardly speak any German - Swiss or not!

The girl spoke English though and I got my chicken and chips okay. I had heard the local Swiss German dialects and accents before but not so pronounced as here in the Kiental. It is a different form of German, more a spoken language then a written one and can differ widely from the language of Germany. All this of course, made little difference to me as whatever accent or form of German I was spoken to in I was not going to understand very much!

Jacqui tells me later on the phone that the forecast for this region is 31 degrees, which is lower than today and going down for the rest of the week. She's also proud of me that I've completed what was one of the hardest days in difficult conditions. I feel better about completing the walk now.

"Tomorrow should be a fairly easy day" I thought to myself as I went to bed. You know those occasions when things don't quite turn out as expected? Well this was one of them.

Chapter Six
A Lone Red Kite

"Buckley! Owen! Kindly stop your warlike activities and try and learn some German!"

Mr Brindley, my school German teacher was referring to Paul Owen's and my pastime of illustrating the German textbooks with scenes from the Second World War instead of paying attention in class.

If, instead of embellishing scenes of the Muller family's life in suburban Essen with Luftwaffe Mescherschmitts giving chase to attacking Spitfires, I had actually paid more attention, I just might have had some idea of what this bus driver was trying to tell me.

I had established that yes, I could get to Ramslaui from Kiental without having to walk all the way but there was something he was trying to tell me about the cable car which was a complete mystery to me as he spoke no English. If I knew what to ask I probably wouldn't have understood the answer anyway and besides, phrases such as "Hold the bridge against the Americans until reinforcements arrive" would do me little good here.

There was no sign of the Australians, maybe they had got on the first bus at 8.20am or possibly they had decided to walk after all. I was on the 10.20 because breakfast, which was included in the enormous room price, wasn't served until 8 o'clock and I wanted to get my money's worth.

Our bright yellow bus wound its way slowly down the tight hairpin bends through the forest on what is the steepest section of road travelled by the Swiss post bus service. Our driver, who was a very friendly and amiable character with a white beard that brought to mind Santa Claus, stopped every so often to talk to anyone who was at the roadside on the way down. Finally we made it down to the valley floor, emerging from the trees into farmland.

There was no modern development in the Kiental valley, it was entirely grassy land with a few old wooden farm buildings and hay barns dotted about, and the only visible occupants were cows and a few goats.

Presently the driver indicated that it was my stop and He now began asking if any of the other half dozen or so passengers spoke English and the bloke sat opposite me said he did. I now learned that the problem with the cable car or *luftselbahn* was that it wasn't actually there. This seemed to me a fairly considerable problem all things being said, but the cables were actually being replaced and there was a minibus that would take me to Ramslauen instead.

The driver got off to retrieve my rucksack from the trailer that these buses tow for such purposes and pointed at a bus in a car park just off the main road. It was not this bus I would need but the small one parked next to it.

He'd been very helpful in ensuring that I knew where I was going and I wondered whether a foreigner in England would be so well looked after by our public transport officials.

I waited in the shade for the minibus to go – there was no-one about and it was already very warm. The valley down here was less rugged than further up – a mixture of sloping farmland and forest. Eventually people started to drift from the village and out of a nearby bar towards the bus, then the driver turned up and we each paid 10 francs and set off.

The journey to Ramslaui or Ramslauen - either name is used depending on which map you have - was not long and we strained up the steep bends on the single track road, sometimes in shady woods and sometimes sunny meadows, arriving in maybe 15 minutes at the berghaus of Ramslaui.
I stopped for the now customary orange juice and ice. This really was an idyllic spot and I was tempted to stay for longer. The place is just out of Heidi – or The Sound of Music – whichever you prefer; with flower filled meadows sloping down to the valley, gentle wooded verdant hills opposite and distant mountains rising to the south. Butterflies were all around on the soft breeze, some of them landing on my table. We don't see so many of them in England nowadays. Soon though it was time to be setting off and accompanied by the scent of wild flowers and sun warmed hay, I began the walk up the hill along a track

following signs for Bachwald. *Wald* means wood and I figured there would be some shade if I went there.

My route led me gently uphill and around to the left before branching right again and entering a dense forest. As I had hoped, a very pleasant and shady forest trail now led more or less on the level, around the contour of the hill. There were occasional views through the trees to the valley far below and then of the still blue waters of the Thunersee to the north as the track curved more to the west.

I had enjoyed walking through the trees as it was cool with an occasional breeze but I was soon back out in the sun again. Passing Bachwald, which was little more than a farm and a large barn occupied by several cows, the path led north again, presently reaching the end of the ridge where it swung west and back down to the south west. Here the view gave the impression of being on the very edge of the Alps. To the south lay the big mountains topped by the Bluemlisalp at over 3600m, its glaciers dazzling in the sun, while north across the mirror like calm of the Thunersee were the foothills. One tall peak, that of Neisen, across the valley, a great, green pyramid rose to over 2300m and was the highest point in that direction, but by and large the land sloped down and disappeared into the lowland plains half obscured under the heat haze.

It felt just as hot as yesterday but I suppose I was much lower here – only 1400-1600m well below yesterday's altitude. My map showed a direct path to Furggi but there was no evidence of this on the ground so I followed the path that did exist downhill to a farm with the strange name of Chueweid, where I joined a track leading back uphill to the left through another meadow. Furggi was basically a wooden hut and I could have reached it much more quickly by heading straight across the field where the other path was supposed to be. Instead it was a steep tramp through swarms of flies that had gathered to harass the herd of cows lazing in the neighbouring field and anyone else who chanced along. There was only me though – and the cows.

There is a high route, the *Nordramp*, that goes along the crest of the ridge to end up closer to Kandersteg but after yesterday I decided that it was too warm to climb a long way in the sun so I decided to follow the path contouring the western slope back to the south and descend to Frutigen in the valley where I could catch a train or bus to Kandersteg. The idea was that this would be an easy option.

At first I followed a wide track of sun-baked mud from Furggi with the Kandertal now visible on my right a long way below. The path descended a little and then climbed across the mountainside passing through areas of trees. I seemed to be following the upper limits of the forest and soon, what I presumed was Frutigen appeared perhaps 1000 metres below in the valley but it was further than I thought to the track leading down to it. The houses and railway yard were seen as from an aeroplane and from this height the traffic moved silently on the autobahn like a line of marching ants.

The path dropped into a hollow in the hillside before climbing over a jutting ridge. It then plunged into thick forest where a short way brought me to another path leading steeply down to the right. This I followed and, emerging from the trees onto steeply sloping alpine meadows, I stopped and finished my water looking down on Frutigen's rooftops far below.

As I headed steeply downhill, the path faded out at times but always it re-appeared lower down. I came in time, to a road which didn't appear to go down to Frutigen so this I crossed at a stile to the right of where I'd emerged and continued downwards, the town not appearing very much nearer. It was hot now and I regretted finishing my water.

A big milestone was passing underneath the power lines which, from up above had appeared half-way down, but soon the slope steepened and entered forest once again. Back into meadows and the obstacles included barbed wire and electric fences, most but not all, having a stile to facilitate crossing. Just as I thought I was almost down, there was a final stretch of almost jungle-like woods which were home to many interesting species of biting and stinging insects, clinging to precipitous slopes.

The path was always there but not many had passed this way and it was overgrown with brambles and other thick undergrowth. I made a note not to wear shorts tomorrow. Not so much for the scratches but I had become badly sunburned above my ankles where I presume my socks had rubbed off the sun cream.

Another forest trail leading down through a near vertical forest and then open grass slopes where the path disappeared without a trace Not to worry - I went towards where I could see a gap in the trees below and there was one last barbed wire fence to negotiate, then houses below in the field.

The track here led straight down to what appeared to be a little village square but was actually on the edge of the town of Frutigen. Its singular most important feature from my point of view was a drinking water fountain.

A short time later, much refreshed, I walked into Frutigen wondering where everyone was. It was deserted, sun baked tarmac with several factories after the houses around the edge. An old woman was cutting a hedge by the roadside – the first person I'd seen since Ramslauen in the Kiental.

"Guten Tag. Wo ist der bahnhof bitte?" I enquired and was given directions to the station that I didn't understand the finer points of. However, I recognised the words *uber die Brucke* – over the bridge - and something about the autobahn, which along with pointing back the way I'd come had enabled me to find the station and a train to Kandersteg just up the valley. There was nothing noteworthy about Frutigen, the place having all the trappings of a transit town that was closed, save for a lone red kite circling over the deserted platforms at the Station.

It had not been the easy day I had hoped for as I walked in the late afternoon sun past several hotels through the small centre of Kandersteg and out on the road towards the Gemmi to my hotel – 10 or 15 minutes from the station. I checked the times to Sunnbuel at the bus stop almost opposite; a quarter past the hour, so I'd aim for 9.15 after an eight o'clock breakfast.

The Hotel des Alpes is a comfortable place for the night and I am welcomed almost like an old friend by the woman who runs the place. The price is most agreeable and I have a shower and relax before having tea which is an excellent pizza on the outside terrace of the hotel.

Much relaxed after the day's ordeal by a combination of pizza and beer, I added to my sense of well-being by giving up my seat to help out the hassled staff trying to find seats for a family who've just arrived. The kids had looked as though they'd start eating each other if they weren't fed soon. I went off to take photos of the small lake behind the hotel that I'd spotted from my room.

The lake is surrounded by reed beds and overhung by the pine forest at one side and after the bustle of the restaurant it is a scene of tranquillity that could almost inspire one to take up fishing. I stay here for a while absorbing my new surroundings.

The Kandertal is different again – back in civilisation after Kiental, the valley is a deep trench like that of Lauterbrunnen but without the snow peaks above. The mountains are of harsh bare rock rising steeply out of the pine forests while on the valley floor are chalets and hotels spread thinly along the road. The road itself extends through the town though most traffic stops at Kandersteg, it being the rail link south. No road crosses the mountains from here. Kandersteg seems a pleasant town and will deserve another visit in the future as I'm too tired for any serious exploration tonight.

Later in the hotel bar, three locals, who resembled Michael Schumacher and his Ferrari team in their matching red and white jackets, arrived and I got talking to one of them whose name was Thomas.

He drunkenly assured me that Kandersteg was the best place to live in the whole of Switzerland – no, the World. He wasn't from here – I think he'd said Zurich – but had moved seventeen years before and stayed. The main reason he cited for his choice of favourite town was the friendliness of the people here. I'd certainly had a warm welcome at the hotel and now I was chatting away to total strangers so I guess he had a point. I was reluctant to leave the warm friendly atmosphere of the bar as I was feeling somewhat homesick again.

Chapter Seven
Walking off the map

That extra couple of beers at the bar hadn't been the best idea I'd ever had but at least I'd left the festivities before I lost the ability to get up for an early breakfast.

The thermometer at Sunnbuel read a much more civilised 15 degrees C and there was more cloud around than yesterday. Ahead lay the wide trail that would take me south over the Bernese Alps, across the Gemmi Pass and off my map of the Jungfrau region. It certainly felt like a major milestone to get out the Kummerley and Frei's Zermatt and Saas Fee edition to replace the one I'd been using on the trip so far.

I'd escaped a hangover but not blisters. I don't usually suffer from them but the long uneven descent yesterday right after the Sefeinenfurka – that and carrying a heavier then normal pack had taken its toll. They weren't that bad – I could walk okay but I'd opted to get the bus from the hotel even though it was only a 5 or 10 minute ride. I wondered whether the driver – who was accompanied in the cab by a small brown dog – was a friend of Michael

Schumacher and Co from the hotel bar. The steering wheel had had the distinctive Ferrari logo in the middle.

For the same reason, I'd also taken the cable car up to Sunnbuel as did everyone else from the bus. The cable car had ascended through some awesome rock scenery with stunning views of the unspoilt Gasteretal which cut into the mountains to the south east, depositing me at the northern end of a vast plateau like valley at about 1900 metres cradled between the jagged peaks and glaciers of the Oberland. This was the Gemmi Pass, one of the most ancient Alpine crossing points. The Gasteretal in fact leads to another crossing point, the nearby Lotschenpass which is a steeper path without the choice of the cable car and crosses to the Lotchental.

The way led slightly downhill at first before heading across the flatter valley floor. The landscape was totally different to that of the Kandertal; the valley was wide, grassy and windswept-looking with few trees, in fact a vast alpine meadow, while either side rock walls rose. To the left the high peaks of the Altels and the Rinderhorn scraped the clouds, huge bluish white glaciers draping their grey rocks, while on the right the valley was walled by a long precipitous rock face that ran its length.

As I pass a herdsman with about forty cows heading the other way, I realise that I'm going okay again, the heat has gone and with it my fatigue. My blisters don't even feel so painful now but I'd still take it easy.

I pass a monument to 6 herdsmen killed when part of the Altels glacier collapsed back in 1895. Looking up, these huge hanging rivers of hard blue ice appear stable but the monument stands testament to the fact that they're always moving, sometimes with disastrous consequences. Soon I begin a gradual ascent. This is wonderful walking country and the scenery is like nothing so far – more like a valley in Norway with its bilberry and heather slopes rising to stark rock peaks, their edges sharpened and polished by the glaciers. The slow climb takes me from the lower valley up a rugged stony barrier to enter a higher one maybe 2 or 300 m above the first. Here I arrive at the berghaus of Schwarenbach where I stop for water. I'm tempted to have a coffee or tea here as it's much cooler now and for the first time since the Schilthorn – that seems ages ago - I put my coat on to sit down.

  The higher valley is narrower and rockier than the first and the path climbs it at an easy angle to reach the Daubensee Lake at 2206m, its chill looking waters stirred into some fair sized waves by a stiff breeze.

  Here I overhear some English voices, the first for some time and get talking to a retired ex-patriot originally from the south of England. He tells me that he lives half the year in Europe, mainly Switzerland and the other half in Hong Kong which is unbearably hot in the summer. I mention that I've not seen many Brits over here this time and he informs me that I'm the first Englishman he's seen in months!

  The main path now went around to the left of the Daubensee and made a climb, which was even easier than the last one, up to the top of the pass at 2322m. Just before the summit an interesting looking path climbed steeply up to the left and I was tempted now that I felt better but I'd promised myself (and Jacqui on the phone) that I'd take it easy today.

The top of the Gemmi is amazing though. The stony hills and rough pastures simply end here as if sliced through with a giant axe. At first sight in fact it appears that the world itself ends here. A hazy distant view of the towering 4000m snow peaks of the Valais across the vast gulf of the Rhone valley far below, and at ones feet, the town of Leukerbad, over 1000m straight down at the base of a sheer precipice.

The pass is not only the Cantonal boundary between Bern and Valais but also the north – south continental divide or watershed of Europe itself. Behind, in the land through which I've been travelling, the rivers drain into the Rhine and ultimately the North Sea whereas to the far side of the ridge they drain into the Rhone which has its outlet in the Mediterranean.

I admired the view for a while but the haze frustrated my attempts to trace my route or identify peaks to the south so headed into the restaurant for a meal of schnitzel. At least I didn't have pizza yet again! The restaurant has huge windows overlooking the abyss and would have a panorama of most of the Rennine Alps –Switzerland's highest range – in clearer conditions.

Now I make the decision to get the cable car down rather than walk to Leukerbad. This is the first of two route decisions that I regret, the second being on the next day.

The path down is well viewed from the cable car, winding as it does down the face of sheer cliffs nearly 1000m high. The route is safe – it's a wide mule track with little danger in good weather – but it looks simply stunning. If I did this route again I'd take an extra day and walk down this way and stay at Leukerbad instead of rushing to cross the Rhone valley the same day.

As I look for the bus timetable at Leukerbad though, I know I've done the right thing. My blisters of that morning seem to have gone – descending that long winding track may have endangered tomorrow's longer stage which should be a highlight of the trip.

I ask someone unloading a minibus by the cable car station where the post bus stop is. It seems I'll need to walk down the road a little way into the village. He speaks good English and enquires where I'm heading.

"Into Turtmann and to Oberems on the cable car," I reply.

"I am going right past Turtmann," he replies in an accent I take to be Dutch. "I can give you a lift there if you like?"

Things are looking up. He has just saved me one of the potential headaches of this trip. I know that I can get to Turtmann but at certain times this may involve catching a train to Visp, then a bus back down the far side of the Rhone Valley, and the cable car onto Oberems is not that frequent. I'd already decided against walking this section as it would take a full day and is mostly on roads and through more built up areas.

By way of thanks, I help him unload the minibus. As well as mountain bikes, it contains some very strange contraptions that resemble children's tricycles with bucket type seats and brakes that look designed for something that can travel at great speeds. He sees my puzzled look and explains that these are a German invention and are designed to be pulled along by huskies when there's no snow for sleds. Or they could be used, if one was so inclined, to plummet down mountainsides when the lack of snow deprives one of the ability to ski. Remembering my injured knee I make a point that if I am ever sat on one of these devices it will be behind a husky on relatively level ground.

Ten minutes later I'm sat in the front of the minibus as Walter, who it transpires is from Belgium, negotiates the steep and winding road down to the Rhone Valley. It turns out that he'd arrived in Saas Fee several years ago and more or less never gone back home. He had a most fascinating job, breeding and training huskies which were much in demand for winter sled rides and summer excursions on some of the machines we'd just unloaded at Leukerbad.

I'd noticed more huskies around in the Alps of late – it used to be St. Bernards that you saw more of – notably at Jungfraujoch and a few at Chamonix. Walter keeps his dogs higher up the mountains, not in the valley, as the heat of the Rhone Valley would, he says, cause them to sleep most of the summer – know the feeling! I mention that they're one of my favourite breeds of dog as they resemble the wolf but I'd heard they don't make good pets.

"Not strictly true," he tells me. "Individually they make excellent pets but do revert to being the pack animal they are in groups – being very like wolves."

We've now left the scented pine woods behind and have entered a brown Mediterranean looking world of sloping vineyards dropping to a sun baked valley floor. The Rhone itself is soon visible meandering in its stony bed below. The temperature is 10 degrees higher down here than at Leukerbad and the warmth and scents of summer have returned as we've descended. The heat-wave may have left the Oberland but it lingers here, more so because of our drop in altitude than our crossing from Northern to Southern Europe though the houses now look Mediterranean rather than Alpine in character. Walter tells me that it's hot all summer down here. Like me, he prefers it cooler than this so stays up in the mountains as much as possible.

Into Turtmann with its white painted houses and our search for the cable car leads us to what was obviously once a cable car station but with no cable – not Rosenlaui again! Stopping and enquiring at a nearby workshop reveals that we need to go around the corner and back maybe half a kilometre. Indeed the cables can be seen climbing the steep hillside above.

I thank Walter again after he's dropped me at the cable car and I investigate the building. There's no-one about and the little ticket office is closed. There is however a telephone so I try and work out what the German instructions mean without much success so I pick up the phone and dial the number on the message anyway. If the police or a fire engine turns up then I'll play the dumb English Tourist who never paid attention in German lessons.

"Where we are here, they might speak French" I think to myself, as I can understand that language much better than German, but to my great relief the man at the other end speaks English. Apparently I am to buy my ticket from the machine and get into the cable car which is a little four man one – it is not locked and will be leaving in ten minutes. This I do!

I think about when I was in this area last summer. I'd been on a train where everyone had been speaking French having come from the French speaking area of Switzerland. When the train had stopped, not far from here, the predominant language suddenly became German, as though a border had been crossed, yet it was only a minor station in the Rhone Valley. The next station, Visp, I got off to change trains and when I went to buy a bottle of water the man in the kiosk addressed me as *Senor!* Italy, of course, is just across the mountains to the South. A strange place is Switzerland.

Clunk! The metallic sound from the door meant I was now locked in. A few moments later there was a beeping sound outside in the deserted station and with a lurch we began to move. Where was the operator? This was a bit too much like Harry Potter for me after a long day!

Turtmann village began to spread out below, swimming pools appearing by some of the houses as they fell away. Presently I was sailing up over rugged slopes leaving the vineyards behind and once again approaching the Alpine landscape I'd become used to. I was joined at Unterems, halfway up, by an old woman with a young girl. We exchanged greeting though she spoke no English. She had a friendly demeanour and asked me a question I didn't understand. As she pointed to my rucksack I realised she was asking if I was going to the Turtmann Hut at the head of this valley.

"*Nein, der Augstbordpass und St. Niklaus,*" I replied, smiling back. She looked impressed – maybe she thought I was headed over there right now! Anyway any thoughts of heroism would have been wiped from her mind when she saw me walk nearly 100 metres from the top station to the Emshorn hotel.

The Emshorn hotel at Oberems is one of my favourite places I've stayed in the Alps – not just on this trip. It costs under £20 for B & B as well! From the hotel terrace 700 metres above the valley floor one can watch the activity below from a safe distance. Cars hurtle along the motorway to the Simplon Tunnel and Italy while on the minor roads people return from offices in Lausanne and Geneva. Up here the only sound is of crickets and the view across the valley to where I've come from today is of a jagged line of peaks edged against the darkening clouds.

My evening meal was Spaghetti Bolognese, which was excellent and I had a good chat with the waitress, whose ability to speak English greatly facilitated my booking a room. Her name, if I get the spelling right, is Fabienne and she had recently spent a month in Bournemouth. I don't know what crime you have to commit here to be sent to Bournemouth for a month but she'd actually enjoyed it, even being keen to go back to England. The only thing she'd not enjoyed was the food. It seemed that the family the unfortunate girl had stayed with lived on nothing but MacDonalds and Burger King and she'd assumed all the English ate nothing but fast food.

After tea I went out to explore Oberems. It was looking like rain so I wasn't intending to go far though as it turned out I was round it in fifteen minutes. It is a delightful place, seemingly untouched by the modern world. The one main street comprises the cable car station, which doubles as a bus stop, my hotel and a large church which looks recent though built in the traditional design. The original church, much smaller, is on through some side streets of rickety looking wooden barn type houses, many of which are raised up from the ground.

Again no-one is about and I get to wondering where all the people are. Many of these villages appear deserted and this was not siesta time. I recall last year when I stopped to eat a sandwich in what was the village square of a similar place near the Trient Valley by the French border. I appeared the only person there when I heard a noise from further up the street. A car was being driven at what was probably its maximum speed all of 200 metres to skid to a halt by the glass recycling bins. A dishevelled looking man appeared from the driver's side and on opening the boot began to unload empty wine bottles into the recycling bin.

He was there over 10 minutes; there must have been hundreds of bottles.

When he'd finished he drove back up to a house at the top of the street and disappeared back inside returning the village to a peaceful silence.

I saw no-one here though, not even the local wine connoisseur with a couple of tons of bottles to dispose of. I went back to my hotel.

Chapter Eight
A Chill in the Morning Air

Despite its remoteness, there are 10 buses a day from Oberems up to Gruben in the Turtmanntal. I was on the one leaving at 8.10 am and in fact was the only passenger. The minibus trundled slowly past the pleasant rustic houses of Oberems which clung to the hillside and entered the forest. This was a bus ride that would go from the edge of modern Europe back a hundred years and into what could have been one of Tolkien's kingdoms.

The single track road meandered under the trees in a pale green morning light. Sometimes the pines parted to reveal untouched clearings below soaring ridges or a steep drop towards the unseen river backed by the opposite slope of yet more trees. There was a rocky gorge below and then an old stone church perched on a precipitous edge. All the time we climbed gradually higher, the mountains on each side growing in stature, hinting at the scale of the giants circling the top of this valley.

Within a couple of minutes I regretted being on the bus. It would have been well worth taking an extra day to walk up this section such was its appeal.

Presently the trees began to open out into wider clearings and swathes of pristine alpine meadow sloped up to screes and crags far above. Further on and the bus passed a couple of wooden buildings and then we came to the end of the road by a small hotel called the *Schwarzhorn*. Just ahead was the small cluster of wooden houses that makes up Gruben.

Here at 1800 metres there was a chill in the morning air. The sound of crickets was long gone and there was not a vineyard in sight, just the path leading up a sloping meadow and vanishing into the kind of forest that in all good stories, bears or wolves used to come out of to terrorise the local populace. Indeed if any still remained in the Swiss Alps it is here they would reside.

I set off up the path past the sign saying Augstbordpass 3 hours and soon entered the forest. This path would take me over the Augstbordpass, which, at not far short of 3000 metres was the highest point of my route to Zermatt. On its far side was St Niklaus in the Mattertal – the valley of the Matterhorn.

This forest trail was a joy. It gained height steadily, the clearings allowing for views up and across the valley to where the hamlet of Oberstafel could be seen below the peak called Bella Tola, which is one of the best viewpoints in the Alps apparently. The track forked once or twice but the branches came back together just being short cuts until I reached a crossroads in the track. To the right went towards the Turtmann Hut by the glacier at the end of the valley while my way led straight across – up the slope ahead.

Soon I was climbing above the trees into the sunlight which had now reached us. The views opened out more and the Oberland peaks I had left behind were visible across the misty depths of the Rhone valley, the Bietschhorn rising as a prominent rocky pyramid.

I was struck by how unspoilt the Turtmanntal is. There is no development or destruction of nature whatsoever. This must be how much of the Alps looked 100 years ago and it should be preserved this way. Perhaps the creation of a National Park would prevent those who would seek to destroy it or would that simply attract too many visitors ensuring the damage would take place anyway. Kleine Scheidegg and Lauterbrunnen were probably once like this.

Continuing upwards, I cross open heathery country before the path slants right across a gravely hillside to reach a signpost informing me that I am now at 2270 metres. The pass is signposted left so I follow this up over open grassland to reach two buildings where I pause for a rest. The silence is total as I gaze out over the upper Turtmanntal to the eternal snows of Les Diablons and Le Tete de Millon across the valley, their glaciers now visible, shining bluish white in the morning sun which is pleasantly warm but not too hot. The wooded valley seems far below now; up here is open country of rough pastures set back from the steep slopes below. Above, a big sky presides over the world of rock and snow.

It's tempting to stay for longer by this sheltering wall but I must go on. I'm enjoying it today though and I press on up the now more gentle slopes towards a jagged line of mountains ahead. Passing a sign indicating my height as 2468 metres is encouraging and I pass a herd of cows grazing in the distance down hill from the path. Soon a small river is crossed and with this on my right I ascend into a more stony landscape. The path now steepens and begins to climb through a large boulder field crossing patches of snow.

Up and up but it's not quite as steep as the Sefeinenfurka was from Murren – and much cooler as well! The forecast had been for 28 degrees C today in the valley and +7 degrees C at 3000 metres which was not far off where the path gets to.

At last a wide stony col and the cairn and a yellow sign saying that this was the Augstbordpass altitude 2894 metres. The view across the other side was of a wild and rugged high country flecked with snow and backed by the 4000 metre Lagginhorn and to its left, the Fletschhorn both across the Mattertal which itself was below my line of sight. A cold wind blew up here, channelling through the rocks of the pass requiring that I put my coat on again to eat lunch.

The descent begins down a gently angled snowfield before winding down amongst boulders. Here I meet the first people I've seen since the bus driver who dropped me off in Gruben. They are a French party of four who are trekking to Evolene to the west of here. I was surprised at how few people there were on this path, it being part of the Walkers' Haute Route from Chamonix to Zermatt, which is a popular long distance trail. I'll have to do that at some stage but this one from Grindelwald to Zermatt is possibly more varied and a shade easier – not having the constant up and down over passes to the next valley day after day.

As I descended in the direction of the snow covered Lagginhorn – which is actually on the far side of the Saas Fe valley, the next one east – the vegetation returned and the boulders and snow patches were left behind. Back in the alpine meadows I passed a herd of sheep grazing near the path and then reached a fork in the track. The bifurcation was clearly signposted and shown on the map. My way led down to the right, towards Jungen and St. Niklaus, heading round to the right of a mountain tarn just below.

Sheep don't seem too common in the Alps. When I walk in the Lake District or North Wales I see them everywhere but, it was Walter I think, who gave me the lift, who had asked if I had seen the herd of sheep on the Gemmi Pass as if they were a curiosity worth seeking out. No, here it's either cows or goats with an occasional wild ibex or chamois – the chamois are the smaller ones I think.

The Jungen/St. Niklaus path led downhill then up a little before contouring the rough mountainside. Opposite, the left fork led down towards the valley but this would have brought me out too far down the Mattertal – somewhere near Stalden. My aim was to head always towards my goal, neither taking any long round about routes nor any difficult direct ones.

I stopped to identify the attractive looking peak above the other trail which looked as though it would make a good walking ascent. The Augstbordhorn it was, and I made a point to climb it at some stage. The path became rough again traversing a wide boulder field which sloped steeply down to the left. The path occasionally faded but could always be found again.

After the boulder field I rounded a sharp corner to be greeted by a wonderful view of the whole of the lower Mattertal, leading down to the Rhone nearly 2000 metres below. The villages spread out on the green patchwork of the valley floor and to the east rose up the peaks of Saastal.

Now there followed a really good bit. The path crossed the steep craggy slope to a second corner which gave a view that was even better than the first. On rounding the corner the panorama opened out right up the Mattertal as well as back down to the Rhone. The top of the valley was dominated not by the Matterhorn but by the Breithorn rising white and cloud topped far to the south. To its right was the towering spire of the nearby Brunegghorn while across the valley the Nadelhorn and Dom were lost in cloud.

I wandered down a little way from the path to where a cairn was perched seemingly on the edge of everything. The valley is perhaps 1600 metres below this peaceful belvedere and occasional sounds from the roads and villages drift up to me from across the vast gulf of air. Here though I remained on the edge of the mountain wilderness I'd just crossed.

The map reveals that this point is marked at 2488 metres and the path to Jungen and St. Niklaus is not a long one from here. A little lower down I meet a walker heading the other way. He's making for Gruben where he's booked into accommodation. He asks how far it is so I ask does he have a head torch. I tell him the path's fairly easy but it's a long way to be setting off at this time and it will certainly be dark as he reaches Gruben. He is aware of the lateness of the hour and was enjoying the view before crossing the path. I tell him about the even better view up by the cairn just above and he thanks me. He has nearly five hours until dark so a concerted effort will get him to Gruben without testing his torch batteries too much.

I wish him luck and continue on down the steeply winding path towards Jungen. As I drop lower and enter the trees again, more people appear on the path and I end up following a family group down a wide forest trail to Jungen perched on a sunny shelf overhanging the last drop to St. Niklaus.

Jungen is a traditional small Alpine hamlet set in meadows where dairy cows graze though a large number of tourists have come up on the cable car and are gathered around a small lake just before the village. I continue to the cable car which is an unmanned one similar to that at Oberems and I ride it down a spectacular drop to St.Niklaus almost directly below.

The noise and bustle of St. Niklaus is an immediate contrast to the Turtmanntal and the Augstbord Pass, even though it's not a busy as Wengen or Grindelwald where I set off all those days ago. I buy a ticket for the cable car I've just been on – yes, kind of after the event I know, but they had no ticket office at the top. Nearly all the people by the lake at Jungen had gone up from here and would return the same way.

I ask directions for my hotel, the Edelweiss, and begin the kilometre or so walk down the road to reach it just down the valley from the town centre. Being on the road feels unnatural and the traffic unfamiliar but St. Niklaus itself does seem a nice enough place. It's quite warm again down here, 27 degrees at the station and I'm looking forward to a shower or bath when I get in.

I check into the hotel which is decorated inside like an old fashioned Alpine lodge with attractive pictures of the well known Valaisian Mountains, including the Matterhorn, despite being on the edge of town. My room is comfortable and I go down for tea outside as it's still warm. I opt for bratwurst, a traditional German sausage for a change and a local beer, which go down very well indeed.

This place is definitely more of a valley hotel reminding me of a place I stayed in Martigny a year ago. Most of the diners have driven here and I don't spot any obvious hikers or climbers apart from one party from Ireland who roll up in a van and unload sacks of gear which they take indoors before returning outside for beer and a meal.

Above the weather is changing with dark grey clouds rolling around the towering rock spires far above. The walls of the Mattertal are exceptionally steep and craggy and tower to a great height on both sides. I'm at the bottom of my earlier view from the cairn I suppose. Despite being near the main road, I decide I like St. Niklaus, It makes a good gateway to the valley of the Matterhorn.

To my great delight lightning illuminates the evening momentarily, like a giant photo flash and the thunder rolls up and down the Mattertal reverberating from the craggy walls. I order another beer and retire to a covered over table to watch the storm just as large drops of rain begin to fall.

Chapter Nine
In the valley of the Matterhorn

As I walked up the road in the sunshine back towards the town centre of St. Niklaus, I was pleased to note that the Hotel Edelweiss had only charged me the 70 francs for a single room – about £30 – instead of the 100 I'd been quoted on the phone. The difference was because they'd only had a double room available but they'd not charged me extra in the end. This put me in a good mood for the morning.

The road to town wasn't ideal walking country but it wasn't that busy and it was a change to see a town that had a life beyond catering for tourists. I passed a builders yard, a sawmill and a warehouse full of what looked to be agricultural implements. A study of the map showed the route to be on the road for some distance the other side of town so I opted to take the train to the next stop and walk from there to Randa, my destination for the day. This would give me an easy day after the Augstbordpass and before the *Europaweg*, the high level trail I planned to follow along its last section into Zermatt.

The sun shone warmly but not oppressively on the pleasant square at the centre of St. Niklaus. Behind the distinctive onion domed church there was an enclosed and sheltered square with what appeared to be a war memorial at one end. Switzerland, of course, didn't get involved in the War and it turned out to be a memorial to the mountain guides of the area who had failed to return safely from the mountains surrounding the Mattertal. There was also a plaque commemorating the British clients of the Guides. The lists of names read like a history of a great battle and brought home how seriously early exploration here was taken and how dangerous these mountains could be.

Wandering around the small town was quite a pleasant experience. It was busy without being crowded, a mixture of tourists and locals going about their daily business. I called into the tourist information office, where a kind lady, who seemed really to enjoy her job, booked me a room at a place called the *Alpenblick* (or Alpine View) for 36 francs or about £15. Even better!

From the train last summer I'd thought Herbiggen looked a nice spot. It was. I was the only person to get off the rather crowded train at its first stop after St. Niklaus and now the train had departed I had the small station to myself. Behind was the sleepy looking village in the midst of a sloping meadow while ahead, over the railway track, the path disappeared into a shady, pine wood. Here lay my walk for the day.

The path led down a short way before crossing the fast flowing river known as the Mattervispa, its water cloudy with glacial sediment. There were signs warning people against attempting to swim here. Quite apart from the fact that the water would be freezing, the river is an outflow for the Grand Dixence hydro-electric scheme and the opening of floodgates upstream can cause dangerous surges of water. Right now the churning river looked capable of sweeping away an elephant and I wasn't tempted one tiny bit to go in for a swim.

On the far side, a leafy path turned left upstream and began to climb into the trees in the direction of Zermatt. It was nothing like as hot as the earlier part of the week but this sheltered valley was much warmer than the breezy Augstbordpass and the shade on this path was very welcome.

After passing a sign for the Topali Hut, which is high up on the mountainside to the right, the path began a gradual descent beneath steep vegetated cliffs with glimpses of the river through the trees below and the open meadows beyond on its far shore. The Topali, in fact, would be an alternative route up this valley. A high level path leads from near Jungen to there and continues up the valley though it would be a long and hard route taking at least one extra day.

Presently I came back to the river and crossed back to the east bank by a footbridge. Here a fairly level grassy track led off to the right up the valley between the river and the railway with the road vaguely heard beyond. It was more open here and the steep walls of the Mattertal could be seen rising for over 2000 metres on both sides. Patchy cloud had formed around the peaks above giving longer spells of shade on what was now quite a warm day.

The route passed the scene of a massive landslide on the far bank; the reason the path was moved onto this side. The slide happened in 1991 and stretches in a massive sweep from the screes far up the mountainside down an unstable looking slope of rocks and shale to end in an unruly tangle of boulders the size of cars and houses right down to the far bank of the rushing Mattervispa.

Travelling up this section of the Mattertal it is not the Matterhorn that dominates the end of the valley but the Breithorn, its glaciers shining white in the sun. The Matterhorn itself is hidden from view further round to the right behind the intervening peaks. Monte Rosa, too, is hidden by the valley walls in the other direction giving the impression that the Breithorn stands on its own.

Up a gradual ascent now past grassy meadows, away from the river and houses appear ahead. I soon find myself crossing a roundabout on the main road and there in front, is Randa. The village makes up for having to cross the roundabout to get here. All the cars are heading further up the valley and Randa's main street is deserted. The houses are all chalet style and most have names painted on the sides, though clearly not all are hotels. This makes it easy to find my night's accommodation the Alpenblick, which is right by the railway station. Another thing I like here is that the houses are well separated rather than huddled together as in some villages giving it a spacious feel.

For £15, my room at the Alpenblick is very good value. It's light and airy and even has a desk by the window where I can sit in comfort and write this. The place is really more of a pension than a hotel though, having a shower and wash room downstairs. There's also a kitchen across the hallway where I can cook breakfast.

The couple who run the Alpenblick are very friendly and helpful too. They are, I would guess, around 60 and moved here from a coastal village in Holland 20 years ago. I comment that you couldn't get two more different places than the Dutch coast and the Pennine Alps which made them laugh.

"But we love the sea almost as much as the mountains. It's just that the mountains won!" I can relate to that.

I spent the rest of the afternoon planning tomorrow's route and having a look round Randa. It's not a big place and the centre is just up the hill from my hotel. Here were a collection of ancient wooden buildings and a stone church dated 1709. It isn't car free, but there was no traffic and hardly anyone about; certainly no tourists apart from me. There was a bonus as well, opposite the church was a sign depicting a cold looking pint of beer, the *Alpen Rose* restaurant. This was the first pub I'd seen so I made a note for that evening.

I then walked to the end of town along a straight, equally quiet, road past a second, much smaller church, to the Dom Hotel, which marked Randa's southern limits and this time succumbed to a pint – it was warm and I'd walked nearly half a mile from my hotel!

The shop I'd passed earlier now appeared to be open so I figured it would be a good idea to get some supplies in for that night and tomorrow as it was the only one I'd seen in Randa.

I'd once read in a really good book about New Zealand called *31 Days in a Campervan*, that many of the rural shops there were like those in England 30 years ago, with museum piece tills and fixtures.

In this one, technology had been abandoned altogether in favour of good old arithmetic. A woman stood at the counter serving customers while a girl, presumably her daughter, added up the prices using pencil and paper. Not even a calculator was in sight.

That evening sees me, quite predictably, back at the Alpen Rose, sat at the table outside the front door with a pint of beer that exactly resembled that depicted on the sign.

I thought about the couple at the hotel and Walter the husky man who'd just upped and moved here. Connie and Benny too from the Lauberhorn hadn't moved country but had come to live in the mountains from the city. If I moved to the Alps I guess Randa was looking favourite so far – I could cope with living here I thought.

Jacqui, my wife, had lived in Switzerland over at Vevey by Lake Geneva working as a teacher. Admittedly Vevey was a town location and she'd been in an apartment but I'd been told of rules and regulations that were comical even compared to some of ours in England.

There was the one where you were allocated a day and time to do your washing which invariably coincided with when you were at work and another stating that it was forbidden to flush the toilet after ten o'clock at night. Can you believe that one! Then there was the Swiss obsession with tidiness with the caretaker of the apartment block rushing out to sweep up the leaves each time any littered his garden – several times a day in the autumn until he'd finally opted to walk around shaking each tree in turn before sweeping the garden. Monty Python would have had a field day with this lot

"I would like a licence for my halibut and special permission to visit the lavatory after ten o'clock."

"Stop that – it's silly!"

The Swiss railways don't seem to have a problem with leaves though.

The evening was peaceful and at the moment I couldn't think of a better spot in which to drink what had somehow become my third pint. Inside, singing briefly broke out – like a cross between yodelling and a German beer drinking song but tuneful enough. A little later a man emerged from the bar and went to tend a cow in its shed next door before returning to his friends.

It's quiet now and the lights begin to emerge in the valley beneath the dark shape of the Mettelhorn. The only sounds are eerie cracks and rumbles from the glacier far above as the ice makes its inexorable journey downwards and a barely audible sound from the motorway below. The cars speed towards Zermatt for that view of the Matterhorn. What are they missing here? Let's not tell them hey?

Chapter Ten
The Europaweg

The 4000m peak of the Breithorn shone in the pale early morning sky like a beacon guiding me on my way. As I followed the road from Randa once again past the Dom hotel, there were stirrings of life from some of the houses which had been quiet the previous evening. It was pleasantly cool down here and the sun would not reach the valley floor for at least another hour.

Beyond the village I walked through flattish meadows and patches of trees. Eventually I came to the main road by a large hotel which was apparently attached to a golf course though I couldn't see it from here. Even the main road was quiet as I followed the wide footpath on its left, alongside the deep shadowed forest. This was definitely a good time for walking. Gone was the heat of yesterday and the colours of the mountainsides above were somehow more vivid as the line of sunlight moved steadily lower.

Leaving the road I followed the path as it slanted off into the trees before emerging once again on the edge of the forest, this time a wide grassy meadow separating the path from the road with the houses of Tasch seen about a mile ahead.

My last memory of Tasch was one of a missed photo opportunity. Last year the train had pulled in at the station on my way back from Zermatt. On the platform right outside my window had been stood a man with one of the most impressive moustaches I had ever seen – a real Kaiser Bill special – they must think it looks cool in Switzerland. He had been stood next to the station sign which read "TASCH". Realising the amusement such a picture would cause, I struggled to get my camera out of my rucksack but alas – as I switched it on the train was pulling away and the shot was lost. This didn't, however, stop a young Japanese man, a couple of rows down the carriage, from racing to get his own camera out and snapping away at the view from the window. He must have taken my action as a cue to take photos though he didn't seem quite sure what of.

Today Tasch was just coming to life. The first tourists of the day were looking in shop windows for something to waste their money on; shopkeepers were eyeing them hopefully, while small trucks loaded with farm produce and fruit raced around seemingly at random. Tasch is larger and busier than Randa but still a pleasant town. It marks the end of the motor road and visitors to Zermatt must catch a train from here to complete their journey. I wander through the main square and turn left up the hill beside a river flowing down from the mountainside above and follow a sign for Taschalp and Europaweg.

As I reach the edge of the town by a steep slope at the limit of the woods I stop and look back over the rooftops. The sun has just arrived in the valley and the day is beginning. The road bends off to the left while the other way a signpost directs to Taschalp and the Grachen-Zermatt Hohenweg up a path between some houses and the steeply sloping forest above.

The Grachen-Zermatt Hohenweg, also more widely known as the Europaweg, is a high level footpath which goes for 31 km or thereabouts from Grachen, above St. Niklaus to, as one would expect, Zermatt. The full route is a two day hike and so uncompromising is the terrain it crosses that the trail is regularly swept by avalanches and stone falls. It is not unknown for parts of the path to be swept away completely in winter or rendered dangerous to cross and be re-routed across the mountainside in a different place when spring arrives.

I would be joining this route a little after the halfway point and following its final section to Zermatt. The first half contains the toughest sections so I would be tackling the slightly easier half. First though I had to get up there to join it, a climb of almost 800m.

As I set off up the path I was preceded for a little way by a blackbird who hopped ahead before pausing and looking back over his shoulder then repeating the process several times as if to say

"Come on, follow me – it's this way." Though the bird's thoughts were probably more along the lines of,

"I wish this clumsy oaf would stop following me and I could get on with breakfast."

The path led on up away from the houses and steadily climbed through the forest, crossing a minor road a couple of times on the way up. The sun glinted in places through the pines in brighter shades of green and the path though fairly steep, was soft and springy with the old pine needles keeping the going easy as I zigzagged higher above Tasch.

After some time I paused at a small shrine above the path and drank some water. The shrine depicted Jesus, not on the cross but apparently giving a sermon. It was a pleasant scene and gave me encouragement – nearly there, not far to go now. On I headed into the woods, always uphill.

The ascent wasn't so bad and I'd stopped noticing the weight of my rucksack. Now there were occasional glimpses of the Weisshorn through the trees across the valley, its peak of rock and ice a grey and white shard against the blue sky.

Presently, I arrived at a clearing where two large crosses had been erected. Here I stopped again and admired my first view of the Matterhorn – or rather it's lower half, cloud having wrapped the summit in grey. This was a peaceful spot with only the sound of birds and the breeze rustling in the trees. I'd seen nobody since Tasch and even any sounds from the valley below were muffled by the surrounding forest. I ate a small amount and relaxed in the sunshine before heading on. It couldn't be much further up to the Europaweg now.

Meeting the road again came as a surprise but I followed it a short distance to a water fountain on the corner. Here a path set off up again into the trees signposted Europaweg, indicating I had 20 minutes to go. This part was steeply up through thicker forest until there in front of me was a wider path cutting across mine. A yellow sign pointed encouragingly right for Zermatt and Sunegga. That was my route.

Once on the Europaweg, the going became much easier again. Mainly because I was no longer going uphill but contouring the slope and the fact that it is an excellent and well maintained path rather like the Eiger Trail where I'd started the route.

I soon emerged from the last of the trees and followed my new found route across the open mountainside. The views here were amazing, the vast scale of the Weisshorn opposite now apparent – at 4505m it's one of the highest peaks in the Alps. Below, the valley of the Mattertal was spread out all the way ahead towards Zermatt and the cloud topped Matterhorn and back down to Tasch below and my route of that morning to Randa, then beyond lay St. Niklaus and the now distant Rhone Valley.

There was a sense of space up here that I'd not felt since being on the Augstbordpass. I crossed steeply sloping Alpine meadows which dropped to the valley's fine detail. The campsite just past Tasch, the road down the valley, the Mattervispa river and the railway partly concealed by artificial tunnels to protect against anything that might fall on it from the precipitous slopes above.

Walking was a pleasure – the path always wide and never too steep up or down. Here for the first time in a long while I passed several parties of walkers and decided to do the full Europaweg route at some stage as it was undoubtedly two days well spent.

Above to the left towered the Mischabel Peaks, the Nadelhorn, Dom, Lenzspitze and Taschhorn all over 4200m, the Dom in fact is the highest mountain wholly within Switzerland (Monte Rosa, they have to share with the Italians) and the path could be seen in front and behind traversing mile after mile of their rock strewn slopes.

Each time the route reached a crest, a little more of the view ahead appeared and now I was looking down on Zermatt itself with the Matterhorn ahead and the familiar skyline of the Breithorn and Gornergrat ridge. Cloud was building up now and the snows had lost their shine, appearing cold and lifeless.

After pausing to eat the rest of my lunch, I rounded a rocky corner to join the path coming down from Ober Sattel (an alternative route on the Europaweg) and continued on towards the half obscured Breithorn. The number of people on the path increased and there below and just ahead was the berghaus of Tufteren I stopped again for the customary orange juice though ice was no longer needed, it being much cooler now.

I relaxed for ten or fifteen minutes on the terrace at Tufteren trying to identify anyone who looked as though they'd come further than the Sunegga railway or even Zermatt. No-one seemed to fit the bill; all were tourists out for a short day hoping for a view of the Matterhorn. No-one was getting that today though; the weather looked to be coming in so I began the last leg of my journey.

Instead of following the signed path directly down to Zermatt, I headed towards Sunegga from where I would walk down through the meadows of Findeln and the woods into Zermatt. This slightly longer route would hopefully be more enjoyable as long as I could complete it before the rain started which it now looked sure to do.

The walk to Sunegga was firstly on a wide track through a forest then over green hillsides with ever present spectacular views. The station looked busy when I reached it but I was able to by-pass it below before following the track to the left which led down to the scattered hamlet of Findeln. This is an idyllic spot consisting of a few small farms and hay barns backed by a wide cirque of meadow beneath the Findeln Glacier which descends from the icy Strahlhorn. Rising on the left were the Rothorn peaks which I'd been up last summer and on the right the ridge called the Hohtalligrat an extension of the Gornergrat, recognisable by the cable car building on its summit.

I resisted the temptation to stop again at a small berghaus in Findeln which I passed after the path had wound back around to the right again. The weather looked thunderous as I left the hollow of Findeln and headed steeply downhill towards Zermatt, the sky surrounding the Matterhorn getting darker by the minute.

Just before I re-entered the woods I stopped to watch two Marmots which were sat on a rock just below the path. They seemed used to seeing people as they didn't run off and hide as they normally do.

The path steepened downhill in relentless zigzags as it made its way towards Zermatt on the valley floor. There were half seen views of the town's rooftops through the trees and as I descended a wooded ridge I encountered the first group of Japanese tourists which suggested that Zermatt was not far!

Following the sign for Zermatt and Winkel Matten I emerged from the trees to cross the Gornergrat Railway and there was the town. I had made it. Only the Matterhorn Trail to do now and that would be when Jacqui arrived in two days – she'd wanted to do the last bit of my walk with me.

Down past the countless apartment blocks – more were being built with groups of ugly yellow tower cranes standing above the rooftops. At least the new buildings were in the traditional chalet style not hideous concrete things but I think Zermatt has surely got enough apartment buildings now. In the days when Whymper climbed the Matterhorn, this place would have been like Gruben or Randa. A certain amount of development was inevitable after the episodes of climbing the Matterhorn and other summits but over doing it can destroy the charm that brought people here in the first place. I conclude though that Zermatt gets away with it – just!

I book into my hotel, the Weisshorn, on the main street. Things are looking up, not only does the room with a balcony cost me less that £20, the restaurant downstairs is a Mexican! Chilli for tea!

It really is amazing. I've walked all (well most) of the way from Grindelwald and though I moaned about it being too hot to start with, I've not got wet once, despite the Bernese Alps having some of the most unsettled weather patterns in Europe. I wasn't getting wet now either, as I sat under the restaurant sunshades drinking my pint watching the rain bouncing off the pavement and forming a fine spray while thunder rumbled up and down the Mattertal. Lightning flickered momentarily through the grey murk above and was followed by a crash as though the mountains themselves were moving. The air grew colder and I decided it was time to return to my room for the evening.

Dawn brought in a low grey ceiling that skimmed the rooftops of the hotels just above the main street. A rest day is in order after all, I feel I deserve one but as the weather is forecast to clear up I can't resist the temptation to go up on the cable car for a short walk up at Trockener Steg. I'd have finished the walk by doing the Matterhorn Trail, but that was for tomorrow with Jacqui, and the route to the Hornli Hut at the base of the Matterhorn's Hornli Ridge which starts the standard ascent route just seemed a bit too energetic.

Along the main street before the bridge there happened a scene from a by-gone age. Out of the windblown fog and drizzle there appeared on the road a large herd of goats. The goatherds were hard pressed to keep their charges from eating every flower and vegetable in sight – bearing in mind the houses of Zermatt nearly all have window boxes. Bells clanking, they passed, heading into town and I continued up the road to board the cable car.

I wasn't in the mood for a long trek or climb today so I spent the morning taking photos of the mountains from the region of the Gandegg Hut. At 3030m it was above the main layers of cloud that blanketed the valley and some atmospheric views were to be had especially from the rocks up behind the hut. Lunch was had with only the ravens for company on a lonely nameless summit high above the Theodul Glacier.

On my return to Zermatt, the weather had improved somewhat and the sun was making tentative attempts to stage a comeback. Zermatt was just the same, busy but not overly so. The tourists on the main street were dressed as if they were going up Everest – just like in Keswick really – but here horse drawn carriages belonging to the resort's plushest hotels transported the rich and their baggage while the trekkers carried their own. The size of the packs some people carried amazed me. I suppose they were camping but I couldn't have managed a lot more weight than I had just carried from Grindelwald.

The electric buggies, taxis and minibuses that charge up and down are a hazard to life and limb. At least though there's not millions of then clogging the streets and the town is free of that awful stench of petrol pollution but because they make no noise you don't hear them coming up behind you so have to jump out of the way at the last minute.

After an evening meal outside at Il Ristorante on the main street – Spaghetti Bolognese again but its good from there and not expensive – I wandered back to my room amazed at what you could actually buy here. Shops sold all manner of trinkets and souvenirs with pictures of the Matterhorn on them. As in Grindelwald where I had started, there were watches, chocolate boxes, cuckoo clocks and cowbells – well it is Switzerland after all - books, maps, climbing and walking equipment (Keswick again) and down near the station I'd even seen a shop with the sign "Baby Shop" in the window, that was taking free enterprise a little too far!

The next morning I was moving hotel to the more up market, but also more expensive, Bellavista, as I was meeting Jacqui at the station that evening. We had a double room booked there for three nights. The Weisshorn had kindly let me leave most of my stuff in the lobby while I went for a short walk in the morning and had lunch which was a bratwurst in a bun from a street vendor in town. Afterwards I carried my re-packed bag down and across the bridge and up the hill to the Bellavista where I checked in again.

I won't bore you with the afternoon's details which were basically sat in the hotel room watching the Tour de France riders negotiate the passes of the Pyrenees live on

Euro sport and trying to work out what had happened from the German commentary

Jacqui was on the train arriving at 7.25pm so a little before then I wandered back down in the direction of the station. Being a little early I found myself looking at some of the watches on offer in an exclusive looking shop. Familiar names; Tissot, Cartier, Rolex; I found myself wondering why the shop had put their phone number on each watch until I realised these huge numbers were actually the prices.

"For that much I'd want to see the engine!" I said out loud. I was pleased to note that the time given by a watch costing more than my car had, was wrong. My £50 Swatch was spot on though and it was time to meet Jacqui at the station.

The 7.25 rolled in at – yes 7.25 - predictable these Swiss trains, though Jacqui later told me that her connection had been late, by almost two whole minutes! We wandered in a leisurely fashion back to the hotel to deposit her bags.

Chapter Eleven
The Long Walk Home

An atmosphere of mystery and calm pervaded at Schwarzsee, the banks of cloud first parting to reveal mountains across the valley then closing in once again to hide them from view. Directly above me towered the jagged rocks of the Matterhorn fading in and out of focus in the drifting mists.

My last time here, I'd wandered up to what had appeared to be a hut – actually the top of a ski run – on a rocky outcrop high above these meadows but well short of the actual Hornli Hut. That time I'd rushed back down to avoid a threatening storm though today the grey clouds surrounding this peaceful setting held no hint of menace.

Jacqui had planned to do the last couple of days of this walk with me though now being 3 months pregnant, long uphill sections such as the Europaweg had been out of the question and as she'd never been to Schwarzsee before, the downhill 10km Matterhorn trail seemed the best place for her to join the walk. It also seemed fitting that I should finish here having started with the Eiger Trail. So it was that on this day of transient views similar to that on which I'd climbed the Schilthorn at the start of the trip we both left the Schwarzsee Hotel and wandered down to the small tarn of the same name.

The tiny white chapel of Maria Zum Schnee or Maria of the Snows stands in a lonely but beautiful position right on the shore of the tarn. It was built in the early 18th century supposedly by two travellers returning over the glaciers from Italy who had, according to legend, become lost and had the chapel built to give thanks for their finding their way back to Zermatt. Before the cable car, this would have been a remote spot indeed.

After walking around the tarn and waiting for the inevitable tourists in bright orange and red coats to move out of the way so we could take our photographs, we both set off down the Matterhorn Trail. This is well signposted and led down a gentle slope descending gradually to the left across open pastures. Here the cloud parted again to reveal the wild upper reaches of the Zermatt valley ahead with its many glaciers framed by jagged grey peaks. There's a path up here to the Schonbielhutte though no way beyond it for the walker, The Col d'Herens to Ferpecle and Evolene being a glacier pass.

On the valleys opposite side, steep craggy walls rose to culminate at the rocks spire of the Obergabelhorn while above and to our left towered the snow encrusted North Face of the Matterhorn, gradually emerging from wind driven clouds. The first ascent of the Matterhorn in 1865 is one of the most documented achievements - and disasters - in mountaineering history and was responsible for much of the early tourism to Zermatt. Father and son Peter Taugwelder senior and junior along with English climber Edward Whymper returned successful to Zermatt while Michel Croz, Charles Hudson, Robert Hadow and Francis Douglas all lost their lives. The North Face was first climbed in 1931 by brothers Franz and Toni Schmid.

The walking trail though has no difficulty at all. Easier than the Eiger trail, the Matterhorn trail descended gradually as a wide track crossing this wonderful open high country before branching down to the right where the mountain bike trail carried on. Eventually the trail descends through an area of vegetation and small trees before curving around into the forest proper and turning back towards Zermatt.

The first stopping point we came to was the rather busy looking Stafelalp but we weren't ready for lunch yet so continued on down through the woods following a wide shady track, now with the Matterhorn's peak behind and to the left.

I was glad Jacqui had managed to join me for the last few days. I hadn't been away for any great length of time but though I'm used to going walking on my own and can manage perfectly well, after a week or so I'd started to miss the conversation and chance to share the day's experiences. I'd not met many English speaking people on the last half of the trail so even the basic conversation as one would engage in with strangers was limited by a language barrier.

Presently we arrived at Furi where we had lunch outside in the sunshine which had gradually returned. We continued after lunch down the path to Zermatt following the route of the cable car. This route headed down the valley on a grassy path that wound down among scattered alp hamlets passing through both patches of forest and meadows before arriving back in Zermatt by the bridge near the cable car station.

The day had turned out bright and sunny with clouds dissipating further and we wandered back to the hotel for showers before heading out to look for something suitably tasty in what had become a fine summer's evening.

The following morning dawned clear and the plan was for me to head up to the Gornergrat and walk along the Hohtalligrat ridge to its summit before returning to Riffelberg part way down from the Gornergrat. Jacqui would catch a later train and meet me there. Being pregnant she didn't want to go much over 2500m and we planned a nice easy walk down to the station at Riffelalp where we'd either get the train down or walk further depending on how she felt. That was the plan anyway. The reality turned out to be somewhat different.

Travelling in the Alps by cable car may be fast and fun especially when it's windy or when they go over the towers but the Gornergrat Railway is the best ride in Zermatt. Reminding me of the Snowdon Railway in North Wales, the trains, electric rather than steam climb the mountain at a leisurely and civilised pace. The journey allows one to contemplate the climatic zones as one ascends from Zermatt at 1600m, through forests then lush alpine meadow around Riffelberg at 2500m, before travelling through the rough sparse pasture of the Rotenboden area to the Alpine stonescape of Gornergrat with its hotel and silver roofed observatory 3080m above the world's oceans and overlooking the ice of the Gorner Glacier.

I briefly went into the small chapel at the summit where many candles burned in the cool twilight before avoiding the crowds by following the track to the left of the hotel and up onto the ridge beyond. The view from here is one of the classics of the Alps and on a day of exceptional clarity like this it was as good as it gets. Below was the Gorner Glacier across which rose the dazzling mass of ice and snow that is Monte Rosa. Beyond the north face of the Breithorn was the Matterhorn's impressive spire then the Dent Blanche, Obergabelhorn and Zinalrothorn. Next was the Weisshorn, an icy pyramid, before the blue white and grey horizon dropped to softer greens and browns of the valley.

To the East the ridge ran in a series of rocky bumps to the cable car building visible on top of the Hohtalli at 3286m. The cable car only runs in the ski season so walking was the only way to reach it today. I set off along the path which passed the turn off right for the Monte Rosa hut actually 300m below across the glacier's flat expanse and followed the ridge in steep little ups and downs to reach a snowfield which required crossing.

Several people had given up at the snow but it was a very short section and not too vertiginous though the snow was frozen and I would have appreciated my ice axe. Once across, the path climbed steeply then crossed a larger but easy angled snowfield before a final steep bouldery scramble led to the cable car building on the summit. Apart from one party of walkers eating lunch the station was deserted. That was despite the view being even better than from Gornergrat which appeared small and far off down the ridge. Below was the Findeln valley I'd walked through on my way to Zermatt, on its far side the Oberrothorn and beyond, the fearsome south face of the Taschhorn.

I relaxed in the sun on the far side where the ridge dropped down before rising to the Stockhorn and the high white plateau beyond; reminiscent of some arctic ice cap except that on its far side was Italy. The silence was total. Here over 2 miles high not a sound broke the stillness. The clamour atop the Gornergrat was far away and I had only the blue vaulted sky and the vast whiteness of the ice fields for company.

Leaving the highest point of my trip, I set off back down the ridge aware that Jacqui would be on her way to Riffelberg by now. I waited by the steep snow field while a Polish family negotiated its crossing. It was clear that they were not experienced and I was terrified that one of the kids would fall off but luckily they crossed okay. While I waited I spotted many wild flowers growing up here among the stones still at over 3000m, before I followed the lower part of the ridge back to the bustle of Gornergrat.

Down to Rotenboden and then the meadows of Riffelberg with its large Victorian hotel appeared below. Last time I was here I'd visited the wonderfully peaceful Riffelsee below the nearby Riffelhorn but now I headed straight to the hotel as I'd arranged to meet Jacqui. She was sunbathing outside the hotel so I decided on a beer. After my sunburn early on in the trip I was avoiding deliberate irradiation. Anyway a beer would be okay; we only had a short walk to go…

Instead of following the railway, we decided on the other main path which descends at first westwards before doubling back down to Riffelberg but finding this closed for repairs, we headed past the modern church which overlooks the Mattertal from a lofty vantage point. This path was longer but would give good views and rejoin the other one lower down. Jacqui was fine with the slight uphill at first as we walked towards the distant Matterhorn on the far side of the valley.

From this plateau of heather and bilberry, the view back down the valley was spectacular with the distant peaks of the Bernese Oberland beyond the hazy depths of the Mattertal and the Rhone valley. All around rose the familiar mountains of Zermatt watched over by the ever present Matterhorn. As the track veered left back towards the cirque of peaks above the Gorner Glacier a change came over the terrain. The gently undulating meadows ceased and on the right the ground fell away to a deep rocky gorge with the glacier and its outflow at the bottom and the Matterhorn rising massively on its far side. Here we looked for the turn off.

Not long afterwards, we were at the junction. Straight on the path headed back up to Riffelsee and the Monte Rosa Hut while a sharp right contoured back below the way we'd come to head around the slope and meet the original route. The terrain was rougher though not hard as we followed the path across the steepening slope with the gorge now on our left, the river churning through the rocks about 700m below.

This was not looking too good. The path was closed again in front apparently for blasting to clear rock falls. We couldn't rejoin the original path. This was most unlike hiking trails in Switzerland where normally plenty of warning is given of obstructions or hazards on a route. There had been no indication at the top that it was closed all the way down and the path could not be rejoined.

Being blown up was not something that was high on either of our lists of "things to do on holiday" so we were left with 2 choices – go back up to Riffelberg and catch the train or descend the steep and rough path down into the depths of the Gorner Gorge and follow the path out to the main valley. It was late, Jacqui was in no condition for anything but easy walking and I'd just done a 3200m peak, had a beer and hadn't planned for anything other than an easy descent.

After some deliberation we decided that continuing down was the better option. We had already descended a fair way and Jacqui was better going downhill than climbing and though the gorge path looked rough and steep, if we took care it would be fine.

"Anyway, I'm pregnant, not disabled!" was Jacqui's current favourite saying and she was an experienced hill walker after all. Besides, the paths here have handrails and steps to aid progress if the going is too steep or loose for the average walker and Swiss hiking trails don't suddenly transform into "climbing routes" without advance warning.

Such were our thoughts as we commenced the long walk home. The path led steeply down in rough switchbacks and was indeed protected in parts by a rope handrail over its early stages. The river could just be heard far below in the rocky defile as we slowly approached it. Part way down we were passed from above on the narrow path by a herd of goats which were being shepherded or rather goat-herded down the mountain. We caught up and passed them again as the path entered a patch of trees which indicated we were getting lower. The goat herd had stopped here to milk one of the goats which had appeared to be struggling with the excess baggage!

The air began to get warmer as we descended into the gorge proper. Granite walls sculpted by ice and water rose above the river while far above glimpses of snow peaks appeared through up at the top end of the gorge.

Ahead could be seen the Klein Matterhorn cable car on its section from Furi to Trockener Steg. I remembered being on the cable car and wanting to explore the path I'd seen winding up into the gorge. It had looked fascinating, probably because it was, though a slightly more planned trip may have been preferable! It is only by walking that one appreciates the true scale of these mountains. Snowdon and Scafell Pike are both around 1000m with Ben Nevis just over 1300m. The summits ringing the top of this valley are mainly over 4000m with the Himalayan scale Lyskamm and Monte Rosa both passing the 4500m level. Just crossing a valley can be a day's walk, climbing a major peak will take 2 days without using the mountain transports and some will take that with mechanical help.

The lower slope down to the river was of boulders and occasional gnarled looking pines. As we followed the river downwards past boulder fields and patches of Alpine flowers in natural rock gardens, huge house sized rocks were balanced precariously in places, left stranded by melting ice. The ones littering the river bank had plunged from the cliffs above. It was a fascinating walk but we both felt a sense of relief by the time we finally crossed the river at a footbridge and climbed a short way up the opposite slope. From here, a wide track led gently down through the pines – a ski run, I think. The sun had gone behind the rock walls above and we began to wonder when the last cable car from Furi was. We were following the line of cables above to reach this station, the one we'd lunched at the day before. Today neither of us really wanted to walk all the way back to Zermatt and it was doubtful whether Jacqui could.

As we both wondered how much further Furi was, the forest suddenly ended and we were back in green meadows with the cable car station just down the hill in front. Thankfully they were still running and we were saved from adding that extra 2 or 3 kilometres onto what had become a bit of an epic day out, if a really good one.

That evening we'd wandered in weary fashion down the steps from the hotel into town for a last meal out before we left on the morning train to Vevey by Lake Geneva. Jacqui's friend Sarah had offered us a bed for the night and we'd get our flight to Liverpool the following morning. The lights of Zermatt were starting to come on as the surrounding mountains darkened, merging into an evening sky that held promise of another fine summer's day.

The tourists were still dressed as if for going up Everest and weary trekkers struggled with the kinds of loads normally transported by Eddie Stobart while speeding electric buggies attempted to run them down. Watches the price of cars proudly displayed the wrong times in shop windows and music drifted invitingly into the street from cosy looking bars. Zermatt was just the same.

As the waiter brought the drinks I commented to Jacqui that today had been harder than intended but we both agreed it had been worth all the extra unplanned effort. This of course was a common sentiment over a drink after the event. Perhaps we were just relieved not to be still stumbling down the trail in the darkness.

Whichever way you look at it though, watching the town around us slowly coming to life for the evening from the comfort of a restaurant terrace, glass of wine in hand, was a fitting end to a long walk in the Alps!